Micro Finance and Economic Empowerment of Women

Micro Finance and Economic Empowerment of Women

Thimmaiya T.D.

ADHYAYAN

ADHYAYAN PUBLISHERS & DISTRIBUTORS

New Delhi-110002

Published by
ADHYAYAN PUBLISHERS & DISTRIBUTORS
4378/4B, 105, J.M.D. House, Murari Lal Street
Ansari Road Darya Ganj, New Delhi - 110002
Ph.: 011-23263018, 011-23277156, Fax: 23280028
Email: adhyayanpublishers@yahoo.com

Micro Finance and Economic Empowerment of Women

Edition 2011
ISBN 978-81-8435-282-5

Printed in India

Published by Harish Chandra Yadav for Adhyayan Publishers & Distributors, Delhi. Laser Typesetting at Jain Computers and Printed at Tarun Offset Printers, Delhi

Preface

The problems of women *workers* are multi-dimensional in character. The problems of women workers differ for considerable extent depending upon the level of education, types of jobs, social equality, working places like rural or urban, agriculture or non-agricultural etc. The level and pattern of women employment is always the indicator of the level of Socio-economic progress. Therefore the problems of the low rate women labour participation is always viewed in the context of the overall problems of the social and economic progress.

Women labour in India in general and Karnataka in particular has not been provided with proper share in work opportunities and even today women being exploited. The economic problems of women, labour range from raising unemployment, low wages, long duration of work hours, stagnant and detracting working condition, sex wise discrimination of wages between male and female workers, absence of job security and irregularly implemented protective legislation like social security, minimum wages, social insurance etc.

There has been considerable increase in the size of women employment both in public and private sector in the country as well as in Karnataka. The economic importance attached to their labour was very marginal. As a result of universal education evolving a new perception about women and her status has increased enormously the number of women in the employment market. As a result of industrial and urban development a greater number of middle class women have found in non-agricultural activities. Female work force and their unemployment at all India level imply not only vast size of female population left as economically non-active . Unemployment has been growing among women in both rural and urban areas of Karnataka.

The ninth plan (1997-2002) document lays emphasis on the participation of the people in the planning process and the promotion of self-help-groups. Empowerment of women is one of the prime objectives of ninth plan. Participatory movement of women is essential for the attainment of women empowerment, which will bring fundamental changes in , economic, educational, political and social sphers. Economic change will possible through women's thrift and unity of credit groups which can create huge fund for loans and credit than what each could ever do alone.

The present study assumes significance in view of its potential to bring into lime - light the constraints and benefits of empowering women at the integrated process of development and social change. Since this study for the first time intends to attempt an estimate of the monetary value of the non-market services render by women within household on the one hand and on the other hand analyze comparatively some selective general women development programmes like Indira Mahila Yojana, Swa Shakti and women development corporation programmes, micro finance programmes etc. In this sense a grass root empirical study of this kind shall be able to throw more light upon difficulties and problems originating at the networking of different women groups as well as implementation of women empowerment programmes. I would like to thank the publisher of Adhyayan Publishers and Distributors, New Delhi for publication of this book in a short period of time.

Thimmaiya T.D.

List of Tables

Table - 3.2	Outreach of Microfinance Institutions in India	42
Table - 3.3	Growth of SHG-Bank Linkage Programme	46
Table - 5.1	Micro-Credit lent by Banks in Karnataka (upto 2008)	70
Table - 5.2	SHG- Bank Linkage - Agency-Wise Cumulative Participation in Karnataka up to March 2008	72
Table - 5.3	SHG- Bank Linkage - Physical & Financial Progress of Participating Regional Rural Banks upto 2007-08	75
Table - 6.1	Other General information of the district	80
Table - 6.2	Block wise/ gender wise population details	81
Table - 6.3	Block wise Literacy details	83
Table - 6.4	Geographical details of Mandya District	85
Table - 6.5	General particulars of Mandya district	86
Table - 6.6	Taluk wise Area and Population of Mandya District (As per 1991 Census)	87
Table - 6.7	Details of Provisional population as per 2001 Census	88

Table - 6.8	The details of Hobli - wise Revenue villages, of the district (Inclusive of up-inhabited villages) - 2001	90
Table - 6.9	Motivating factors-Members perception	92
Table - 6.10	Members perception on assuming leadership role	100
Table - 6.11	Reasons for abstaining from leadership	101
Table - 6.12	Agency-wise distribution of members by age group	102
Table - 6.13	Agency-wise distribution of members by family size	102
Table - 6.14	Agency wise distribution of members by religion	104
Table - 6.15	Distribution of members by social status	106
Table - 6.16	Distribution of members by level of education	107
Table - 6.17	Group-wise activity status of beneficiaries	108
Table - 6.18	Activity Status of beneficiaries	110
Table - 6.19	Distribution of members by monthly family income	111
Table - 6.20	Members perception about factors contributing to groups success	114
Table - 6.21	Members' perception on factors preventing groups further growth	114

Abbreviations

IRDP	Integrated Rural Development Programme
JSY	Jawahar Samridhi Yojana
EAS	Employment Assurance Scheme
SHGs	Self-Help Groups
NABARD	National Bank for Agriculture and Rural Development
DWCRA	Development of Women and Children in Rural Areas
NGIs	Non-Governmental Institutions
BGB	Bangladesh Grameen Bank
BMNP	Basic Minimum Needs Programme
NREP	National Rural Wage Employment Programme
SSP	Stree Shakthi Programme
PLDs	Primary Land Development Banks
WID	Women in Development
ZP	Zilla Panchayath,
RMK	Rastriya Mahila Kosh
UNO	United Nation Organization
TRYSEM	Training of Rural Youth for Self - Employment
RBI	Reserve Bank of India
WCDD	Women and Child Development Department

SJSRY	–	Swarna Jayanthi Shahari Rojgar Yojana
LBS	–	Lead Bank Scheme
RRBs	–	Regional Rural Banks
MRD	–	Mysore Reconstruction Development
CDS	–	Community Development Society

Contents

	Preface	v
	List of Tables	vii
	Abbreviations	ix
1.	Introduction	1
2.	Review of Literature	19
3.	Micro Finance Programmes in India - An Overview	28
4.	National Policy for the Empowerment of Women	49
5.	SHGs and Micro Finance Programmes in Karnataka	64
6.	Micro Finance Programmes and Socio-Economic Development of Women - Case Study Analysis	77
7.	Summary, Major Findings and Policy Implications	121
	Bibliography	131
	Index	142

1

Introduction

The Setting

In 20th Century the term 'Women Empowerment', 'Women Welfare'. 'Gender Justice' have come in lime light in the social, economic, and political development analysis of both developed and developing nations. Traditionally women in almost every society had remained second grade citizen. Social network also made women dependent of men in all spheres of life right from birth to her last rites. In actual terms women had become slaves of men, whose sole aim was to use them for bearing and rearing up children and fulfilling their sexual desires. Neither they were allowed to get themselves educated nor they were given legal rights in the property, and in administration. Their freedom and status were exploited by marrying them in tender age and keeping them inside the house, exploiting their labour and dignity to maximum possible extent and at last force them to get themselves bury alive with the dead body of their husbands.

The situation took turn with the spread of liberal ideas of the west among the Indian people as well as in other third world countries. The new intelligentsia's were convinced that the new society could politically, culturally and economically develop only on the basis of liberal principles such as the recognition of individual liberty, freedom of unfettered expression of human personality and social equality. The newly educated persons increasingly revolted against rigid social conventions and out dated customs. They could no longer tolerate irrational and dehumanizing social practices. In their revolt they were inspired by the humanistic ideals of social equality and the equal worth of all individuals. This class of Indian society had taken lead during the nineteenth century in the religious and social reforms, which gave birth to the empowerment of various segments of the society.

Social movements propelled the 20th Century's progress towards equality regardless of gender, race, religion, ethnicity or age. One of the most significant has been the movement for women's rights, with roots back over the centuries. The issue of empowerment of women becomes more significant because women constitute half of the population and unfortunately they had been discriminated a lot.

Women in India had a respect in the family and the society during pre-Vedic and Vedic age. Sucheta Kripalani states, "That in Rig-Vedic age, the women of India enjoyed and exceptionally high status. At that time women were not only their husband's life-long partner and companion in weal and woe, but also the mistress of their household and real partner in all their activities, including religious sacrifices. Women's entry into their husband house was regarded as an auspicious event bringing blessings to the entire household. Her high education was regarded as a necessary accomplishment for being well placed in life.

Situation took ugly turn in the Post-Vedic age. The girls lost the status of 'dwija' and came to be regarded as 'Shudras'. Basically it was Manu who often quoted for disparaging women and relegating them to the lowly status. By the close of the ancient period women's social and domestic life had generally suffered a radical change and they had come to occupy position of inferiority both at home and in society.

Arrival of Muslim invaders and their rule over a large part of Indian sub-continent made the women's position and status worse. Women were deprived of education, free movement, basic human rights and privileges.

Before the colonial era social status of women in India was pitiable as is reflected through following incidences:

- A female birth was considered a curse on the family. In many parts of India the parents or 'Dai' - The traditional birth attendant, killed newly born female babies.
- To save the young women from sexual exploitation by the feudal lords, they were kept in 'Parda'. Custom of early marriage and 'Parda Pratha' was the result of this very reason.
- The 'Sati Pratha' was prevalent through out the India. Widows who refused to become 'Sati' were forces to live an in - human life.
- Education was not regarded the right of women.
- Taking meals, women were last in the Queue.
- Women were treated like a commodity.
- Wife had no right to decide the size of her family, to buy or sell property, to visit her relatives freely or to help someone economically.

Empowerment of women is a global issue and it is an active, multidimensional process, which enables women to realize their full identity and powers in all spheres of life advocated by international organizations like United and its constituent Commissions on women, United Nations developmental programmes, International Labour Organisations on one hand and world conferences on women at Mexico (1975), Nairobi (1985) and Beijing (1995) on the other hand during the last two decades.

The phrase "Empowering women" denotes social, economic, cultural and political empowerment of women vis-a-vis men. In other words, empowering women implies abolition of all kinds of male bias against women or gender discrimination against women or gender inequalities in different walks of life. In simple women empowerment as a social goal implies the existence of total inequality between female and male members. This problem of gender in equality is ubiquitous. It differs only in degree and it manifesto itself in different varying forms, across different societies in the contemporary world.

Empowerment can take place at a hierarchy of different levels-individual, household, community and societal and is facilitated by providing encouraging factors (e.g., exposure to new activities, which can build capacities) and removing inhibiting factors (e.g., lack of resources and skills). Two vital processes have been identified as important for empowerment. The first is social mobilization and collective agency, as poor women often lack the basic capabilities and self-confidence to counter and change existing disparities and barriers against them. Often, change agents are needed to catalyze social mobilization consciously, second, the process of social mobilization needs to be accompanied and complemented by economic security. As long as the disadvantaged suffer from economic deprivation and livelihood insecurity, they will not be in a position to mobilize (UNDP-2001).

With the above brief conceptual understanding of empowerment, what strategies can be used effectively to empower women? In many developing countries (especially in South Asia). One strategy, which has been found to be promising, is participatory institution building in the self-help groups, often coupled with savings and micro credit loans. In India (especially in Karnataka) women development Corporation is doing good job in this regard.

In most of the developing countries today, more and more emphasis is laid on the need for development of women and their active participation in the main stream of development process. It is also widely recognized that apart from managing household, bearing children, rural women bring income with productive activities ranging from traditional work in the fields to working in factories or running small and petty businesses. They have also proven that they can be better entrepreneurs and development managers in any kind of human development activities. Therefore, it is important and utmost necessary to make rural women empowered in taking decisions to enable them to be in the central part of any human development process. The empowerment of women also considered as an active process enabling women to realize their full identity and power in all spheres of life.

Micro finance is a significant factor and accessible to small and Micro enterprises, Socio, economic, cultural progress of poor women. Education and training also plays a major role in changing the life of poor women. So the future of SHG's partly lies in the overall growth of mainstream rural finance, on one hand and the increases in self and group entrepreneurship activities on the other hand of this, the second factor depends on the high growth potential of the Indian economy in future. The Indian poor definitely deserve the enlarging opportunities in social banking. The Government of India should not view microfinance as a close substitute for programmes of rural development and/ or poverty alleviation schemes in future.

In sustaining the development of the rural area, credit is playing a key role. Primary sector will continue to play an important role in the national economy to meet the increasing demand of a growing population and the industrial sector. Rural development thus depends on the amount of credit available in rural areas.

In the Indian banking system rural banking has become an important segment. After nationalization of banks in 1969, they forced to move towards rural India and open their branches to meet the credit requirements of rural mass.[1] As a result about 50 percent of the bank branches are located in wide spread rural area. The concept of class banking has changed its dimension and now the concept is mass banking. In the context of rural banking so many steps have been initiated by the Government of India, such as bank nationalization, Lead Bank Scheme, setting up of Regional Rural Banks, creation of NABARD, implementation of service area approach etc.

As we know that, in unorganized sector indigenous bankers, money lender are still playing their own role. They provide timely and quick loan facility, but charge high rate of interest varies between 24 percent to 60 percent per annum and even more. In organized sector commercial banks, regional rural banks and cooperatives are meeting the credit needs of the people in rural areas, where nearly 643 million people living in 5.76 lakh villages out of the total 1027 million people residing in India. Though these institutions are functioning in good number, large number of ruralites is not exposed to and accessed the services offered by them. They are deprived of these services and left behind. The main reasons for this are illiteracy, ignorance, security problem, cumbersome and lengthy procedures followed by the banking institutions etc. [2]

In the emergence of micro finance or micro credit system the inability of credit institutions to deal with the credit requirements of the poor effectively has led an important role. Credit is a crucial input in the process of development. Micro finance provides credit access to poor with no collateral obligations. It encourages savings and promotes income-generating activities. Loans are provided at the market driven rates of interest and peer pressure is used in repayment. Micro finance is carried out through self help groups where poor come together in the range of 10-20 by weekly, fortnightly and monthly meetings through their savings and loaning. It is hoped that through such interventions hitherto uncovered groups are covered with credit and in the process get empowered.[3]

In spite of the massive scale of government intervention towards rural development in India, rural India continues to be reeling under poverty and related problems. Not withstanding the phenomenal progress seen in the rural credit structure in terms of volume of credit extended, concessionality, coverage of weaker sections including scheduled castes and tribes, almost all institutions constituting the formal part of the rural credit system, suffer from several shortcomings like; (a) Gap between the concern of the policy makers and the quality of the effort (b) Defects in policy design (c) Infirmities in implementation (d) Loans to the poor were considered as a part of social sector lending and not commercial (e) It was felt that poor were not borrowers but beneficiaries (f) An attitude of 'carefully disguised cynicism towards the poor' and (g) An attitude of 'poor are not bankable'.

This possibly has been due to the absence of the people's participation in the development programmes and also due to the gap in mutual understanding about perspectives of the supply side (the government, planners. and the bureaucracy) on the one hand and the demand side (the rural poor) on the other. This gap is felt to be filled by the microfinance activity through the Self Help Group approach for sustainable rural development.[4]

The significant feature of the Self Help Groups [SHGs] is that they provide credit to the poor at unsubsidized interest rates besides having relatively low default rates on these loans. SHGs reduce transaction costs of financial institutions that do business with the poor and that of the SHGs themselves. They reduce the cost of financial institutions by acting as intermediary organizations or by providing social collateral that substitute for costly loan appraisals and supervisions. SHG approach has made considerable impact on the development of rural economy in terms of increasing savings of the poor, providing access to credit for the poor at reasonable rates of interest by establishing linkages with the formal financial institutions, improving the production levels and income levels, increasing food security and standard of living, improving asset creation and enhancing income generation activities, augmenting environment sustainability and contributing for the much needed women empowerment. With the enthusiastic roles played by the NGOs, the banks, the public and the governments, over a period of one and a half decade, the SHG approach has transformed into a movement in the rural areas. [5]

Self Help Groups have been receiving greater attention by all the concerned like the Government, NABARD, RBI, Commercial Banks, and RRBs. This innovative form of credit delivery is catching up in a big way in rural areas. SHG movement is leveraging the strength of the formal banking system and flexibility of informal SHGs in providing adequate financial services to the rural poor. The programme has turned in to a social movement with high expansion rates in recent years. Fuelled by competence and enthusiasm at all stakeholder levels, it is expanding rapidly throughout India, including tribal areas. [6] It is probably the world's largest and most successful micro finance programme for the rural poor-outstanding in its emphasis on self-reliance and local autonomy of the very poor. It is widely felt that there have been perceptible changes in the living conditions of the rural poor mainly on economic side and relatively on social side. It is with this perceptional background that a detailed study has to be undertaken to find out the economic impact of the Self-Help Groups on the development of rural economy.

In this context, it is desirable to generate information and analyse to what extent these Self Help Groups have been able to reduce poverty and vulnerability by; increasing capital / asset formation at the household level, improving household and enterprise incomes, enhancing the capacity of individuals and households to manage risk, increasing enterprise activity within households, expanding employment opportunities for the poor in non-farm enterprises, empowering women and improving the accessibility of other financial services at the community level.

Micro-finance aims at providing the rural and urban poor, especially women, with savings, credit and insurance facilities to set up or expand income-generating activities, and to improve household income security. The micro-finance programmes, as we shall discuss below, are expected to alleviate poverty and empower women.

Empowerment is a process by which women take control of their lives through expansion of their choices. Thus it is the process of acquiring the ability to make strategic life choices in a context where this ability has previously been denied. The core elements of empowerment have been defined as agency, awareness of gendered power structures, self-esteem and self-confidence (Kabeer - 2001). The empowerment process must organize women into collectives, breaking out from individual isolation and creating a united forum through which women can challenge their subordination. [7]

Empowerment can take place at a hierarchy of different levels individual, household, community and societal and is facilitated by providing encouraging factors and removing inhibiting factors. In 20th Century the term 'Women Empowerment', 'Women Welfare'. 'Gender justice' have come in lime light in the social, economic, and political development analysis of both developed and developing nations. Traditionally women in almost every society have remained second grade citizen. Social network had so women as to keep women dependent of men in all spheres of life right from birth to her last rites. [8] In actual terms women had become slaves of men, whose sole aim was to use them for bearing and rearing -up-children and fulfilling their sexual desires. Neither they were allowed to get themselves educated nor they were given legal rights in the property, and in administration. Their freedom and status were exploited by marrying them in tender age and keeping them in side the house, exploiting their labour and dignity to maximum possible extent and at last force them to get themselves bury alive with the dead body of their husbands.

- In this backdrop, exploring the rationale behind the evolution of micro finance institutions as an alternative source to meet the financial requirements of the poor and studying institutional objectives, structure and approaches in meeting their financial demands, needs immediate attention as well as further research.

Micro finance in general is a practice of providing the poor with credit, savings and insurance facilities to set up or to expand Income Generating Activities relating to agriculture and its allied activities and non-farm sector, and thereby is poverty reducing mechanism.

Micro finance is needed a very traditional and familiar form of business. Microfinance has turned out to be useful development assistance product. It reached millions of poor people and emerged as a revolution. It is a viable alternative that reached the hitherto unreached for their social and economic empowerment through financial and social intermediation. In microfinance the practice of group-lending contracts with joint liability is widely accepted as a potential innovation or a noble solution for imperfections in rural credit markets to minimize risks in the credit markets. The joint liability between the group members provides incentives or compels the group to undertake the tasks of selection, monitoring and enforcement of repayment in a cost effective manner. This leads to reduced transaction costs, increased volume of transactions and improved accessibility of credit to the poor.[10]

The institutional arrangements that are providing financial services at the micro level are called Micro Finance Institutions (MFIs). Asian Development Bank defines MFIs as "Institutions whose major business is the provision of micro finance services. MFIs have been operating under different legal systems and structures like non-profit MFIs, Cooperatives, Registered Banking Institutions, and Government Organizations. The most significant observation made by Hulme and Mosely (1996) is that the Non-profit MFIs or NGO-MFIs have comparative advantage over the profit institutions in providing the formal sector financial services to the poor. Many of the pioneer MFIs working in the world today like Grameen Bank, BRAC (Bangladesh), and SANASA (Sri Lanka) , KREP (Kenya), MMF(Malawi), Banco Sol (Bolivia) are basically NGOs. Subsequently, some of them have transformed into banks or they work on the lines of NGO-MFIs on a large scale. There are a large number of unregulated NGO-MFIs in the world of micro finance; they count for 61.4 percent of the sample.

Grameen Bank and Bangladesh Rural Advancement Committee are the two important MFIs that emerged first in South Asia. Later, the Bangladesh Grameen Bank model was replicated in more than six other countries in Africa and Asia. In 1986, Nepal adopted the new strategy of linking SHGs with the formal financial institutions. In pursuit of this, in 1988, Indonesia started linking banks and SHGs. Following Indonesian experience with MFIs, countries like Philippines, Thailand, Sri Lanka and India in the early 1990s too initiated micro level financial services for the rural poor with different institutional structures.

Statement of the Problem

The poverty in India has a strong gender dimension. In order to develop and empower women, the government has been formulating policies and programmes, which have been operationalised through five year plans since independence. A review of the policies and programmes is undertaken during and at the end of each plan period while preparing plan documents. Such a constant review, based on evaluation and studies conducted on government initiated women development and empowerment programmes, and the successful programmes of civil society organisations within and outside the country, together with political mobilization of women, have resulted in the following changes:

- A shift in policy focus from welfare to development

and to empowerment during the five-year plan periods, especially after the 1970s.

- Assignment of functions relating to women's development and empowerment to different types of local organisations, line departments, local government, NGOs and others.
- Mandatory representation of women in the decentralized government at the district and below.
- Formation of grass roots level women's organisations for their development and empowerment.
- A shift in targeting strategy from 'individual beneficiaries' to 'self-help groups of women involved in micro finance.
- A shift in strategy from issuing loans to individual beneficiaries to using micro-finance as an instrument for development and empowerment of women organized in SHGs.

Micro finance programmes are expected to make a significant contribution to poverty alleviation and empower the members in economic, social and political spheres. These programmes are also expected to become increasingly self-reliant and independent of donor funds. Recent studies, however, question this enthusiasm. While one group of studies argues that micro-finance has very beneficial social and economic impact, others caution against such optimism. Other studies suggest that beneficial impact of micro-finance programmes; but argue that micro-finance does not assist the poorest thus questioning the ability of the programmes in targeting the poor, the sustaining of the services provided and the ability of the programmes to reduce poverty. The studies also note that there are only limited data on the impact of NGO programmes on poverty and that NGOs comparative advantage over other service agencies needs to be investigated rather than assumed. Thus, it appears that micro-finance programmes have not always succeeded in their objectives of sustainable poverty alleviation and empowerment.

NGOs are building social capital in the form of groups that can generate a sound base for their members to develop their credibility as borrowers and encourage financial institutions to develop confidence in establishing a lending relationship with the groups. Thus, NGOs transform the beneficiaries into borrowers leading to establishment of systems and structures in which a sustainable process of linking the poor borrowers to sources of capital and other financial services with formal financial institutions is achieved. There is little doubt that support for microenterprise has dramatically increased since the late 1980s. This study critically examines the credit-initiated microenterprise development of the NGO as a strategy to promote poverty alleviation. Satisfactory through the performance of the NGO is in ensuring access of the poor, particularly poor women, to institutional sources of credit, and alleviating poverty to some extent.

With this background, the study seeks to examine the functioning of micro-finance programmes, and analyze economic benefits (improvement in livelihoods and access to resources) and social benefits (improvement in knowledge and participation) of the selected micro-finances on members in the specific context of NGO programmes in Mandya district. The study also looks at the lessons from the selected micro finance programmes, and examines the likely pointers on what could be the possible trends in economic and social benefits. The policy suggestions have been provided at the end.

Scope of the Study

The present study is an attempt to examine the economic viability of different financial institutions in Karnataka in general and in depth enquiry is restricted to NGOs, Self Help Groups sponsored by banking sectors and state government. The study mainly throws light upon the costs of credit, profit, income, saving and employment creation of the SHGs through micro finance. However, the factors that influence the viability such as profitability, in case activity and efficiency of micro finance institutions and infrastructure have also been incorporated in order to promote rural development programmes and poverty eradication and employment generation schemes. The study focuses on the NGO-Micro finance and socio-economic development of women. It is assumed that the study will help the policy makers and others to devise suitable policies for the success of various categories of the NGOs situated under micro finance and SHGs in the State in particular and the country in general. It is hoped that the findings of the study will provide stimulation and insights for further studies in the NGOs based microfinance and SHGs.

Objectives of the Study

The main focus of the study is to examine the role of micro finance and its impact on socio-economic development of beneficiaries from Self-help Groups and Non Government Organizations. The specific objectives of the study are as follows:

1. To evaluate the extent of influence and support of micro finance institutions in implementing microfinance programmes for upliftment of women.
2. To examine the employment activities of Self-Help Groups under micro credit programmes in the study area.
3. To study the role of Self-Help Groups in socio-economic empowerment of women in Mandya district.
4. To evaluate the problems being faced by the SHGs in implementing the micro-credit programmes
5. To suggest appropriate policy measures based on the findings, which emerge from the proposed study.

Hypotheses of the Study

The following are the hypotheses formulated based on the review of existing studies

1. Micro-Finance Institutional facilities are promoting saving, credit, and income generating activities of the poor people.
2. Employment is increasing due to Microfinance activities of SHCs.
3. Non-government Organizations and Government microcredit programmers are supporting to upliftment of the poor.
4. Self-Help Groups are an effective instrument for development initiative of the poor people.

Methodology of the Study

The present study is an empirical investigation based on sample beneficiaries of microfinance institutions in Mandya district of Karnataka. The present study is based on both secondary and primary data and a systematic random sampling method has been adopted for survey. The primary data has been collected from Mandya district.

The sample size comprised of 186 beneficiaries from microfinance activities in the Mandya district of Karnataka State. The present study has selected two taluks in the district for the purpose of primary data collection. To have further clarity, Graphs, pie-charts and diagrams have been worked out.

Sources of Data

A planned approach has been employed for data collection so that the facts that are near to reality and free from aberrations are elicited for impact evaluation. The data have been collected mainly from secondary sources. The secondary has been collected from the NABARD's publications, Bank's publications and other governmental/ non-governmental organization publications. Secondary data are collected and processed by some other agencies on the subject of SHGs. Some of the sources of secondary data are:

- various publications of central, state and local governments
- existing literature and data in websites
  various publications of national institutions like NABARD,RBI, NIRD, NIBM and other agencies
- other sources like books, magazines, newspapers, reports, articles, seminar papers published by universities and research institutions.
- ZP Office Mandya.

Chapter Scheme of the study

The present study consist of seven chapters, following is the chapter scheme of the study:

Chapter- I : Introduction

The first chapter is introductory in nature and spells out the statement of the problem, importance of the study, scope of the study, objectives of the study, and the area and period of the study. This chapter also deals with methodology and plan of the study, sources of data. This chapter serves as the foundation on the basis of which the other chapters of the study are developed.

Chapter - II : Review of Literature

The second chapter represents the review of literature relating to women development programmes, SHGs and Micro Finance and finally identified the research gaps based on the review of the previous studies.

Chapter - III : Micro Finance Programmes in India - An Overview

The third chapter deals with micro finance programmes

in India. In this chapter Mainstream Microfinance Institutions, Alternative Microfinance Institutions and National Policy on Micro-Finance, and Guiding principles of RBI on Microfinance.

Chapter - IV National Policy for the Empowerment of Women

This chapter deals with national policy for the empowerment of women in India. This includes an overview of the national policy and other components.

Chapter - V : SHGs and Micro Finance Programmes in Karnataka

The fourth chapter represents the SHGs and its emergence in Karnataka and attempt has also been made on the role of SHGs in micro finance. A detailed analysis is made on micro finance programmes in the state of Karnataka.

Chapter - VI : Micro Finance Programmes and Socio-Economic Development of Women - Case Study Analysis

This chapter deals with NGO micro finance programmes and its role in socio-economic development of women in Mandya district of Karnataka. This chapter is the core chapter of the present study. A detailed field survey analysis has been presented in this chapter.

Chapter - VII : Summary, Major Findings and Policy Implications

The last chapter sets out a summary, and presents the conclusions of the study. It also attempts to indicate the changes in the procedure and pattern of the micro finance programme, which called for the fuller realisation of the objectives as originally envisaged.

References

1. Rathnakarachary Thumoju (2009) Rural Credit Delivery System: A Study, Southern Economist, Vol.48 No. 4, 2009.
2. Basu.P (2006) Improving Access to Finance for India's Rural poor. Washington: The World Bank.
3. Subbalakshmi.A.V.V.S (2009) Micro Finance: A Study of Sample Blocks of Kancheepuram, Southern Economist, Vol.48, No.4, 2009.
4. Rajasekhar.D (2002a) Impact of Micro-Finance Programmes on Poverty and Gender Equality: Some Evidence from Indian NGOs. Kumarian Press.Inc.
5. Shrivastava, Deepa. (1987): Role of women in Economic Development of India, Annual Conference of Indian Economic Association, Rajasthan University, Jaipur.
6. Raj Kumar Sen (1998): Optimizing the Role of Human Beings in Economic Development. Women and Economic Development, Discovery Publishing House, New Delhi.
7. Mahajan .V.S. (1989): "Women's contribution to India's Economic and social development" Deep and Deep publication, Delhi.
8. Devasia Leelamma, Devaisa V.V. : (1994): "Empowering women for sustainable development" Manpower Journal, Vol. XXI Oct. Dec.
9. Bhatia.V.K.(1986):"Some Empowering Dimensions of Women Work Force", Manpower Journal Vol.XXII,No.2,july-Sep,p.31-44.
10. Atmanand (1990):"Women Labour force: Trend and Pattern Employment". Khadi Gramodyog, Vol.XXXVI, No.6,Mar,P.247-54.

This excess in demand of capital can be met with the help of loans. Providing credit (loans) to the rural poor to meet the legitimate needs and expand their opportunities in the prime requirement.

The Development School came in for a lot of criticisms by the scholars belonging to the 'Banking School'. Profound scholars belonging to Banking School like Dale Adams, Von Pischke, Douglas Graham, Gordon Donald argue that credit does not play a leading role but a facilitating role in the process of economic development. Some of the problems that the scholars identified with the traditional credit model are, limited out reach of credit failure of the credit institutions to sustain themselves financially.

Thus, rural credit policies in low developed countries are not supportive to increase productivity in addition to reducing poverty. The decades of 50s and 60's were marked with the supply of credit, which were seen as important constraints for economic development by many developing countries. Thus, it was widely believed that providing accessibility to credit to the rural poor was considered essential to alleviate poverty and promote economic development. Although informal credit markets operated widely in rural areas, high interest rates of money lenders hindered the process of investing in productive income activities by the rural poor (Von Pischke 1983).

The National Government, Donors, Multilateral Financial Agencies funded credit programmes for the rural poor through various financial institutions at subsidized rates (Padmanaban 1988). The subsidized credit lending discourages the underprivileged from saving as they provided low rate of interest (Von Pischke 1992). The low rate of interest in the rural credit market leads to excess demand for loanable funds. Excess demand for credit caused credit rationing by the lenders. The subsidized credit to the rural poor in developing countries did not result in the desired goal of poverty reduction. Government subsidized credits were labelled as credits that hardly reached the poor, generated economic rents, in efficiencies

2

Review of Literature

This chapter deals with the brief review of previous studies on self help groups, microfinance and empowerment of women. Here an attempt is made to review the theoretical studies and empirical studies on empowerment of women.

Theoretical Framework

There are in a broad sense, both micro and macro economic foundations of the theory of institutional economics. The theory of institutional economics is an important part of theoretical welfare economics. The theoretical arguments regarding the role of finance in poverty alleviation are broadly classified into two main views, the 'Development School' (Lipton 1998). The Development School views that lack of credit is a major constraint in taking up productive activities. It believes that there is a need to steer rural credit into productive projects and into the hands of the rural poor. Ragner Nurks argues that the underdeveloped countries are plagued with vicious circle of poverty due to low productivity, low income, low saving capacity and vice versa. Similarly, Arthur Lewis in his "Theory of Economic Growth" (1995) argues that the poor in rural areas need much more capital than they save in order to invest in productive activities.

and financially unsustainable. In general, the past performance of the state or donor sponsored rural finance operation has fallen short of expectations.

The Conventional (subsidized) Credit Model was subjected to serious criticism from the mid - 1970s as donor and multilateral agencies switched their attention from 'state intervention' to 'market - oriented' solution. Changes in interest rate, policies and saving mobilization became the cornerstone of new thinking regarding rural financial markets.

The break down of the system gave rise to new awareness among the economists, policy makers and donors in order to look beyond the present credit model and take on a board about the need of institutional viability and efficient allocation of resources. Thus, the Banking School Model emerged as an alternative to the Traditional.

Mellor and Desai (1993) proposed the 'structuralism view' by stating that inappropriate organizational structure of financial institutions was a major reason for poor performance. Generally, financial institutions provide that of 'credit alone' services, which have not contributed to economic development in general and poverty alleviation in particular. This view prompted the 'credit plus' approach in development banking and led to the promotion of Multifunctional Financial Institutions which were encouraged to provide credit along with non-credit services to the poor.

Hoff and Stiglitz (1990) and their followers were instrumental in presenting what is known as the 'Information Paradigm'. This paradigm primarily emphasized the problem of information asymmetry in the rural credit market. This asymmetry characterized by three interrelated situations, viz., adverse selection, moral hazard and enforcement. Operation of these mechanisms cause rationed credit and segmented credit markets.

The group based lending which is practiced in Micro Finance Institutions can overcome fundamental barriers of financial intermediation between lenders and borrowers.

The reduction of transaction cost for both the lenders and borrowers has the potential to lower these barriers there by increasing credit services to the poor in a more sustainable manner (Von Pischke at 1983, Hulme and Hosby 1996). The success of Micro Finance Institutions like the Grameena Bank, Bancosol of Bolivia, the BRAC and Indonesia, the SEWA in India and many others have been attributed these innovations in the provision of financial services. The institutional innovations have lowered the cost and risks of making loans to the poor due to social collateral, savings promotion and ensuring sustainability.

Empirical Studies

The empirical studies are applied research studies. They help us to test the theories or models and also provide insights to reformulate old theories and models and/or formulate new theories and models.

Shylendra H.S (2008)[1] in his study on "Role of self-Help Groups", has stated that- there is a massive, Mobilization of women taking place as a result of the SHG moment. The growth of SHG in accidentally has occurred during the economic reforms period.

The SHG Movement has a good potential to serve both as well as contribute towards women's emancipation. There is a major onus on all actors involved in SHG promotion and development to further intensify their efforts in enabling SHGs to reach a nature stage. We need a major investment in capacity building of SHG and product policies to help over come constraints faced by SHG integrate them fully into developmental programmes. S riraman U.P (2006)[2] in his study on Micro Finance Self-Help groups and women Empowerment-current issues and cancerns analysed that-"Even though there were Many benefits due to Micro-finance towards women empowerment and poverty alleviation, there are some cancerns First, these are dependent on the programmatic and institutional strategies adopted by the intermediaries.

Second, there are limits to how far micro-credit interventions can reach the ultra poor. Third, the extent of positive results varies across house -hold headship, caste and religion and Fourth, the regulation of the both public and private infrastructure in the context of LPG to suction the benefits of social service providers".

Sabyosachi Dos (2003)[3] in his study on " Self-Help groups and Micro-Credit", observed that Micro credit is an alternative source of credit, Most important input for development, to the poorer section of the society but also aimed for their capacity building. The phenomenal growth of SHG indicates that the weaker sections of the society also capable to sharpen their micro-entrepreneurial skills with the help of their own savings and additional bank credit as needed. At this point Micro credit-SHG integration could be the way out for overall rural development vis-à-vis poverty alleviation.

Kumarn K.P (1997)[4] in his study on "Role of NGO in formation of self-help groups, Empowerment of People Gross roots strategies and Issue" opined that-flexibility of SHG in meeting the credit needs of the poor women related in the women using the health and howling by woman have to be understand as investment for better living.

The intervention by NGO and group strategy has resulted in cultivating the women for saving and borrowing in the group. The collective bargaining strength has increased the confidence of poor to like the IGA for augmenting their earring capacity, Hence, it is concluded that group approach as mode the home to learn to earn in the village itself. This is a most important welfare consequence of the self-help among the women.

Arjun Y. Pangannovar (2009)[5] in his study on "Rural Development Women Self-help Groups", observed that a self-help group is an informal association of rural poor women who have come forward voluntarily to work for their economic, social and political development. It provides the rural poor with the means of economic and social entitlements. In more precise way; the rural poor women and brining about of rural development through their efforts to eradicate rural poverty in particular and the all sided sustainable development of the country in general.

Archna sood (2004)[6] in her study on "Sustainable rural development" analyzed women self-help groups; to improve the social, economic and political empowerment of women and to help these who have become victims of the development process and who struggle to conserve their sustenance base, women empower themselves by forming autonomous groups. These women empower themselves by forming autonomous groups. These groups mobilise women's intent energy and teach them to earn their own living. Thus women led SHG to the main stream of decision making, SHG is a viable organized set up to disburse micro credit to rural women, encouraging them to enter into entrepreneurial activists, as women prove to be very good entrepreneurs.

Archana Sinks (2004)[7] in her paper on "Micro finance for women's empowerment" analyzed Micro- credit on micro-finance for women has received extensive recognition as a strategy for poverty reduction and for economic empowerment. Questions are often asked whether micro-credit is the most effective approach to economic empowerment of the poorest and among them, women on particular. Development practitioners often argue that the poor has neglected by the state and public institutions in addressing employment and livelihood needs. This article puts forward a debate on micro-credit for policy-makers, researches and development practitioners.

Rimishim Moulumi Dos (2004)[8] in her article on "Micro finance through SHG" analyzed the access of poor to credit is the biggest need of the hour rather than cheaper rate of interest. Micro finance provides opportunity to the poor for getting sufficient amount of credit easily to start any income generating activity, Micro finance not only deals with savings and insurance part. It ensures the right to save and it is one of the most powerful weapons, which works for bringing the poor rural people into mainstream.

Pillai J.H (1995)[9] in his study "Women and Empowerment" analyzed that Empowerment is an active, multi-dimensional process, which enables women to use their full potential and powers in all spheres of life. Power is not a commodity to be transacted, not can it be given away as loans. Power has to be acquired and once acquired it needs to be exercised, sustained and preserved. Empowerment is a process of literally means becoming powerful in short, empowerment is a process of challenging existing power. Empowerment is attained through awareness and capacity building leading to greater participation. In decision making process, control and transformative actor.

Marilee Harl (1995)[10] in his paper on "Women's economic empowerment in South Asia" analyzed that empowerment is a process both individual and collective since it is through involvement in groups the women most often begin to development their awareness and the ability to organize, to take action and bring about change.

The group approach to poverty alleviation implies strengthening of collective self help capacities at the local level to enable in line with the poor to plan, manage and monitor their access to assets to overcome their vulnerable situation or to undertake based on self help principle are emerging as alternative mechanism to empower them.

Guru Murthy.T.R (2000)[11] in his study on "Self-help Groups Empower Rural Women" analyzed empowering women contributes to social development. Economic progress in any country whether developed or under developed could be achieved through social development, women's contribution to national development is crucial. The process of economic development would be incomplete and lopsided unless women are fully involved in it. Emancipation of women is an essential pre-requisite for economic development and social progress of the nation.

Murugan K.R and B.Dharmalingam (2000),[12] in the joint

study of "Self-help groups new women's movement" examined empowerment of women through self help groups would lead to benefits not only to the individual women and women groups but also for the family and community as a whole through collective action for development. These groups have common perception of need and an impulse towards collective action. Empowering is not just for meeting their economic needs but also meeting holistic social development.

Tamil Mani. B (2002)[13] in his article on "People Centered Development Projects through PRA" analyzed development programmes of different types designed and implemented have enhanced the socio-economic conditions of the down trodden. Many programmes do not succeed as people's voice is often ignored. Participatory approach must be introduced at all stages as we are really concerned with people's empowerment. As this approach brings the people to focus the project activities.

Ashok Kumar Mishra (1999)[14] in his study on "Self-help Groups and Social Defence" analyzed the programme to link the rural poor with the rural main stream institutional system through formation of self-help groups (SHG) has taken shap micro-credit innovation in the rural credit dispensation mechanism in India. The emergence of SHG as a forum of the poor has no doubt helped in strengthening their horizon.

Research Gaps

The above studies reveals that, the self-help groups are an important social infrastructure which has significant influence on economic development as well as human development. The study on socio-economic empowerment of women through Micro Finance in Karnataka with special reference to Mandya district is first of its kind. In Karnataka so far no study has been made to analyze the role of government programmes in socio-economic empowerment of women. Hence, to fulfill that research gap the present study is undertaken.

References

1. Shylenra H.S. (2008) " Role of Self-help Groups", Yojana, January 2008.
2. Siraman. V.P. (2006), "Micro Finance, Self-help Groups and Women Empowerment Current Issues and Concerns", Working Paper 38.
3. Sybyolachi Dos (2003), "Self-help Groups and Micro Credit", Kurkshetra, August 2003.
4. Kumaran. K.P. (1997), "Role of NGO in promotion of self-help groups, Empowerment of People: Gross Roots Strategies and Issues", Kurukshetra March 1997, pp. 40-46.
5. Arjun Y. Panogannovar (2009)" Rural Development; Women Self-help Group, Southern Economist march 2009, pp, 19-20.
6. Archna Sood (2004), "Sustainable Rural Development" Kurukshetra, April 2004.
7. Archana Sinha (2004), "Micro finance for women's empowerment", Kurukshetra, April 2004.
8. Rimishim Mousumi Dos (2004), " Micro finance through SHG Kurukshetra, February 2004.
9. Pillai J.K.(1995) "Women and Empowerment" Gyan Publishing House, New Delhi, 1995.
10. Marilee Karl (1995) "Women's Economic Empowerment in South Asia, Vistar Publications New Delhi, 1996, pp. 191-292.
11. Gurumurthy T.R.(2000), Self-help Groups Empower Rural Women Kurukshetra vol 48, No.5.
12. Murugan K.R and B.Dharmalingam (2000), Self-help groups new women's movement", Social Welfare, vol. 47, No.5, August 2000.
13. Tamil Mani. B (2002) " People Centered Development Projects through PRA" Kurukshetra, vol 50, N0.3 January.
14. Ashok Kumar Mishra (1999) Self-help Groups and Social Defense Social Welfare, 44(10), pp. 30-3.

3

Micro Finance Programmes in India – An Overview

In this chapter an attempt has been made to review the Micro Finance Programmes in India. Analysis is started with brief background of the evolution of Micro Finance.

Background

Micro-credit or micro-finance is a useful tool in building the capacity of the poor in management of sustainable self-employment activities. Microfinance provides opportunity to the poor and weaker section of the society for getting required amount of credit on easy terms and conditions to start any income generating activity. The Task Force on Supportive and Regulatory Framework for micro finance in India defined micro finance as the "provision of thrift, credit and other financial services and products of very small amount to the poor in rural, semi-urban or urban areas enabling them to raise their income levels and improve living standards". Under micro credit system, there is no dearth of financial resources as well as problem of repayments. Through this system the credit can be channelised and made available to poor individually or in groups. Self help groups emerged as the alternative delivery mechanism. [1]

Micro finance will be an alternative model for development. It helps in income creation, asset creation and employment creation. Micro credit has been receiving a significant amount of attention all over the World, especially in developing countries. It is felt that by providing micro credit to the "poorest of the poor', the gap in the formal rural credit sector can be filled. A majority of such projects are now being controlled by non-government organizations in the hope that they will be able to overcome the weakness in the banking system. However, while small-scale rural credit is necessary, overall credit policy must build on the strengths of the banking system in India as its mainstay.

In the 1920s, Malcolm Darling remarked that the "Indian peasant is born in debt, lives in debt and dies in debt" (Darling 1925). Sixty years after independence, this is still true. The National Sample Survey (NSS) on the situational assessment of farmers undertaken in 2003 reported that on an average 48.6 percent of farmer households in the country were indebted, with the percentage being as high as 82 percent in Andhra Pradesh.

Micro-finance is widely regarded as an innovation having the potential to minimize risks in the credit market. Microfinance implies providing the poor with savings, credit and insurance facilities to set up or expand income generating activities relating to agriculture, allied activities and non-farm Sector, and thereby, increase household income security. A group of about 15-20 members provides Microfinance services. The members periodically contribute savings, which are used to build a savings fund that can be revolved among the members. The members are encouraged to borrow from the savings fund thus created to meet their consumption and short-term production needs. Since this fund, built entirely on the savings of members is normally insufficient to finance income generating activities involving larger amounts of start-up capital, the micro- finance groups are linked to formal banks to obtain bulk loans for on-lending to group members.

The credit fund comes from an outside source is disbursed to individual members according to an agreed criteria and the group undertakes joint liability for the debts of each member. Alternatively, funds may be lent by an external agency to individual group members, and the joint group guarantees all the loans. The joint liability provides incentives or compels the group to undertake the tasks of selection, monitoring and enforcement of repayment in a cost-effective manner, leading to reduced transaction costs, increased volume of transactions and improved access of the poor to credit. For this to happen, the group should be small and homogenous, and have access to incentives. The joint liability works better in communities characterized by close social ties and social capital, and in remote areas not having access to alternative sources of credit (Sharma and Zeller 1997).[2]

Microfinance covers the delivery of banking and other financial services at affordable costs to the vast sections of disadvantaged and low-income groups. Easy access to public goods and services is essential for an open, inclusive and efficient society. Micro finance in India, presently provides mainly savings and credit facilities under different models, viz (a) the banks providing "no-frills" deposit facilities, remittances, insurance and small loans; (b) the self-help group bank linkage model; (c) the microfinance institutions model; (d) the post-offices, one of the most widespread organisations in the country, with 1,38,000 rural offices have also been providing small savings, remittance facilities and postal life insurance facilities. Micro finance has had a tremendous impact on the lives of the underprivileged rural people. [3]

Evolution of Microfinance

The NABARD has successfully spearheaded the microfinance programme through partnership with various stakeholders like non-governmental organisations (NGOs), banks, cooperatives, etc., in the formal and informal sector, with support from both the government of India and the

Reserve Bank of India, since the early 1990s. The SHG bank linkage programme was launched by NABARD as a pilot project in 1992 against the backdrop of a huge banking structure unable to adequately address the microcredit needs of the poor. Encouraged by the positive results of the pilot project, the RBI advised banks in 1996 to mainstream the SHG bank linkage programme. The programme acquired national priority from 1999 onwards with successive union budget pronouncements. The programme has since come a long way from the pilot stage and has clearly emerged as the primary model for providing rural microfinance services as a proven method of extending formal financial services to the unbanked rural clientele. This is a home-grown model, very flexible and without any dependence on foreign funding.

The microfinance institutions are an extremely heterogeneous group. Registered as non-banking finance companies, societies, trusts or cooperatives they employ a variety of ways to ensure microcredit delivery. Even as the SHG method was being fine-tuned, many NGOs were using a variety of delivery mechanisms for providing microcredit services with financial support from external donors and apex institutions including the Rashtriya Mahila Kosh, Small Industries Development Bank of India and NABARD. Since 2000, commercial banks including RRBs and a few cooperative banks have been providing funds to microfinance institutions for on-lending to poor clients. The role of NABARD in the growth of the microfinance model has been multidimensional, as under: (a) policy formulation; (b) financial innovations; (c) technological interventions; and (d) institutional strengthening.

The microfinance programmes are considered to have the following potential to address problems of the poor, in general and women, in particular. Lending to the poor is considered to be costly and risky because of thin low savings propensities and inability to provide collateral. Microfinance groups, however, target the poor better as the joint liability compels these groups to be small and homogenous so that members have incentives to participate in selection, monitoring and ensuring the repayment of loans. This implies that the groups can be formed for the poorest as the households with similar characteristics (savings capacity, credit needs, etc.) actually contribute to their success. The highlights of microfinance are the following:

1. Micro-finance programmes enable the poor to save.
2. As the amount of members savings at the disposal of the group increases, the member households can withdraw savings or take credit for consumption, which leads to reduced dependence on moneylenders, food security, and enhanced access to health and education.
3. Microfinance groups improve access of the poor to credit.
4. Access to production credit enables them to undertake income-generating activities through which poverty can be reduced.
5. Credit for poor to undertake income-generating activities enable them to have access to resources and income.
6. Repayment rates are expected to high in microfinance groups having dynamic incentives such as each successful repayment leads to larger loan amount
7. The income generating activities enable poor to have access to income, and enhanced decision-making on health, education, consumption, etc.
8. The SHGs, promoted for the poor people, especially women, enable them to develop leadership qualities, enhance self-management, and facilitate them to be self-reliant. These also strengthen the individual and collective decision-making, and bargaining.

Regular savings by enabling the people to develop confidence and introducing them to local banks contribute to improved creditworthiness of the poor. This would enable and improved interface between banks and people's institutions.

There are several microfinance-implementing organizations that provide small loans in India. Some of them have successfully expanded their services to thousands of borrowers. Given the fact that most of these borrowers would not have had access to formal financial institutions, that many of the borrowers utilise the loans to enter or expand their informal sector micro enterprises, and that the informal sector continues to be an important source of livelihood for many poor people, these Micro Finance Organizations may very well have had a major impact on improving the living standards of millions of poor persons as well as on promoting economic growth.

Three types of sources provide microfinance services- formal institutions, such as rural banks and co-operatives; Semiformal institutions, such as NGOs, and Informal sources such as moneylenders and shopkeepers. The different organizations in this field can be classified as "mainstream" and "alternative" micro finance institutions.

Mainstream Microfinance Institutions

Apex level institutions like NABARD, Small Industries Development Bank of India (SIDBI), Housing Development Finance Corporation (HDFC), Commercial Banks, Regional Rural Banks (RRBs), RMK the credit cooperative societies, etc., are some of the mainstream financial institutions involved in extending micro finance and they have played an important role in promoting micro-finance operations in the country by providing financial assistance in the form of grants, loans or revolving fund assistance to the NGOs. Till such time the credit institutions are able to meet the capacity building costs of the NGOs, they may have to continue providing financial support. In the long run, however, the bank has to meet these costs from their own resources, which will accrue to them due to the reduction in the transaction and risk costs. Some of the NGOs have promoted formal micro-financial institutions by having off their credit activity to exclusively focus on providing micro-financial. In the case of such MFIs, refinance could be made available on the same terms and conditions as applicable to other credit institutions. It will be necessary to make a clear distinction between NGOs performing the role of SHPIs and those rendering direct financial intermediation for the purpose of providing financial support.[4]

Capacity building of the poor as well as trained manpower is crucial to the success of upscaling of micro-finance in the operations. Although efforts have been made to identify the NGOs, which could act as resource center for training of the poor and the bank personnel, these efforts have to intensify through a cohesive approach in policy. Co-ordination is required between the NGOs and federation of SHGs, government agencies and apex financial institutions in promoting micro-finance in the country.

Alternative Microfinance Institutions

These are the institutions, which have come up to fill the gap between the demand and supply for micro finance. The MFIs can be broadly classified as: NGOs, which are mainly engaged in promoting SHGs and their federations at a cluster level, and linking SHGs with banks, under the NABARD scheme. NGOs direct lending to borrowers, who are either organised into SHGs or into Grameen Bank style groups and centers. These NGOs borrow bulk funds from RMK, SIDBI, FWWB and various donors. MFIs, which are specifically organized as cooperatives, such as the SEWA Bank and various Mutually Aided Cooperative Thrift and Credit Societies (MACTS) in Andra Pradesh. MFIs, which are organized as Non-Banking Finance Companies, such as BASIX, CFTS, Mirzapur and SHARE Micro, fin Ltd.

Some of the leading alternative micro finance institutions in this segment are SEWA Bank in Gujarat, which also runs federations of SHGs in nine districts; ASSEFA and its Sarva Jana Seva Kosh Ltd., and ASA in Tamilnadu; SHARE, BASIX, CARE and MACTs in Andrha Pradesh promoted among others by the Cooperative Development Foundation, MYRADA in Karnataka, which has promoted Sanghamitra, a company of its village savings and credit sanghas; PRADAN, which has established a large number of SHGs and federated them under Damodar in Bihar, Sakhi Samiti in Rajasthan and the Kalanjiams in Tamil Nadu (the last now run by DHAN Foundation); ADITHI in Bihar, which has established Nidhi, a federation of women's groups. PREM in Orissa has done the same through the Utkal Mahila Sanchay Bika; the Rashtriya Gramin Vikas Nidhi which runs credit and savings programmes in Assam, Orissa, on the lines of the Grameen Bank Bangladesh, as does SHARE in PASA in Tamil Nadu and RDO in Manipur.

National Policy on Micro-Finance

There is a strong case for formal recognition of Micro Finance just like institutional credit as a strategic tool for poverty alleviation and rural development. The National Policy on Micro Finance should emphasize on encouraging initiatives and participation of different types of institutions in microfinance, bringing the micro finance activities irrespective of the type of institutions involved within the regulation and supervision by competent authorities. Creating policy environment for closer linkages of the microfinance sector with the formal banking channels, and making available equity start up capital and capacity-building funds for the existing and prospective institutions engaged in microfinance. The recommendations of the Task Force are intended to address the above components. The main objectives of the National Policy on micro finance are as follows:

- Encouragement of micro finance efforts and Micro Finance Institutions
- To bring all microfinance activities under the supervision and control of strong authority
- Creation of bank linkage environment to microfinance system
- Attraction of institutional investment towards micro finance sector
- Promotion of all type of financial services including insurance
- Extension of social security fund network to all microfinance activities/ clients
- Microfinance institutions and workers in microfinance should be act as institutions of social security system of the Government.
- Preparation of scheme to protect all types of small savers in MFIs.

Reasons for Introduction of Micro- Finance in India

The insufficient availability of credit from the Formal Rural Banking System (FRBS) for the rural poor and the consequential adverse impact on agricultural productivity and incomes has been the concerns of policymakers and academics in India. The nationalisation of banks in 1969 brought an increase in the number of branches in rural areas and in the various policies aimed at social banking. This has improved rural people's access to credit. Nevertheless, the inequalities, in the banking system across the regions and social classes, persisted. The number of the poor (in particular women) obtaining credit from the Formal Rural Banking System (FRBS) was lower and it should have been expected considering their proportion within the population. This was because of the following:

- Insistence on collateral, which could not be provided by the poor and especially women.
- Complicated administrative procedures.
- Long distances between the villages and the bank branch.

- Inflexible lending policies and procedures.
- Lack of credit available for consumption.
- A widespread belief that the poor are non-bankable.

Although some of the rural poor obtained credit from the FRBS, they found that credit was neither timely nor adequate for their needs. Furthermore, the purpose for which an application for loan was made, and the entrepreneurial experience of loan applicants was not considered when loans were ultimately sanctioned. Without a sufficient understanding of the purposes for which loans were taken, borrowers tended to utilise the loan for purposes other than income generation. There were also problems within the FRB system such as lack of complementary business support. This led to the following responses:

Firstly, there was mounting pressure on the government from Indian bankers and some outside agencies to undertake finance sector reforms so that the banking sector could become financially viable. Yielding to this pressure, the government appointed the Narasimham Committee in 1991, which recommended measures to improve the viability of the financial sector. One recommendation was that, the priority sector lending should be gradually reduced from 40 per cent of the total advances in 1994 by ten per cent every year until it could be removed altogether. This would have further reduced the availability of credit to the poor. However, the government did not accept this recommendation, and even stipulated that foreign banks should continue to provide credit to all social classes. Even so, the proportion of credit provided to the priority sector declined from 37.7 per cent in 1991, to 28.9 per cent in 1996. Although banks attributed this to a decreased demand for priority sector credit, a time-series analysis of trends in agricultural credit flow arrived at the conclusion that the banks were diverting credit to more profitable areas .[5]

Secondly, in the wake of increasing transaction costs, mounting overdue payments and widespread criticism relating to social banking programmes such as Integrated Rural Development Programme (IRDP), the Indian banks started showing considerable interest in group-based credit programme of Development of Women and Children in Rural Areas (DWCRA). The commercial banks were particularly attracted to this programme because lending was based on the savings of women members, and larger loans would be given only after the group had proved itself through repayment. Loan assistance to women's groups was found to be relatively more productive than other social banking programme, and repayment rates were better. The government agencies such as District Rural Development Agency (DRDA) and Integrated Tribal Development Agency (ITDA) provide funds to DWCRA groups formed by both government officials and non-governmental organisations (NGOs).

Thirdly, the Indian government decided that, from 1999-2000 onwards, group methodology should be adopted in the case of poverty alleviation programmes. Consequently, a new programme of Swarnajayanti Grama Swarojgar Yojana (SGSY) was formulated to combine the erstwhile poverty alleviation programmes such as IRDP, TRYSEM and DWCRA. This programme channelled the assistance to those poor who were part of a SHG. The SHG would select the beneficiaries, and help the implementing agencies in monitoring the assistance provided and help in the recovery of loans, if any.

Fourthly, commercial banks tried to find ways of improving their financial viability. In addition to the reduction in the amount of priority sector lending and the provision of recycled short-term credit, banks lent to the members of SHGs, which undertook the responsibility of selection, monitoring and recovery of loans, and repayment to banks. Banks lending to SHGs not only obtained refinance from the National Bank for Agriculture and Rural Development (NABARD) but also had the advantages of a "reduction in the transaction costs, improvement in recoveries and profit margins lending to wider coverage of the target group". This was corroborated by studies, which showed that banks' transaction costs were less, under the programme, as the burden of selection, monitoring and recovery of loans was passed on to the NGOs and SHGs. The borrowers also experienced a reduction in transaction costs. The banks' financial commitments were also less in this programme than in social banking programmes such as IRDP. In the case of IRDP loans, the ratio of bank credit of NABARD's refinance was 3.8:1. On the other hand, in the case of credit given under SHG-bank linkage programme, the ratio of bank credit to NABARD's refinance worked out to be 1.1:1 (NABARD 1997).[2] As the amount of NABARD refinance depended on recovery performance, a lower ratio in the case of SHG-bank linkage programme indicated that recovery rates were high in this programme. As a result, the number of SHGs linked to banks increased rapidly from 255 in 1992-93, to 8,598 in 1996-97. In 1997, 29 commercial banks, 79 RRBs and 12 co-operative banks participated in the programme in 18 different states. An estimated 1.5 lakh member family was covered.

Fifth, rigid banking systems and the consequent inaccessibility of credit to the poor stimulated many NGOs in introducing and expanding micro-finance programmes. A majority of the estimated 30,000 NGOs in India started micro-finance programmes. The government even formed programmes such as Rashtriya Mahila Kosh (RMK) through which SHG groups formulated by NGOs could access credit and other support. Quasi-government agencies, such as NABARD and the Small Industries Development Bank of India (SIDBI), also formulated programmes to link micro-finance. This was due to the growing role of NGOs, within micro-finance, which raised questions with regard to whether their services were complementary to or substituting the FRBS.

Some of the critiques argued that the total amount of credit provided by the microfinance programmes formed only a small proportion of credit provided by the FRBS, as the loan amounts offered by microfinance programmes were smaller. Therefore, it was argued that microfinance programmes could not play a significant role in poverty alleviation. The proponents of NGO microfinance programmes argued that NGO credit programmes provided a reliable source of credit to the poor, helped them meet their consumption credit requirements, reduced their dependence on moneylenders, and improved the collective strength of the poor in approaching government agencies and in accessing resources from them. They argued that although micro-finance programmes could not substitute the Formal Rural Banking System, they did enable the poor to save, and provide the poor with the confidence to approach banks to deposit their savings, thus allowing them to access the bank's other resources. The proponents argued that a linkage process between the NGO, its members and the FRBS, would not become sustainable if the poor developed linkages from a weak position. Therefore, micro-finance programmes were adopted as the strategy to strengthen the position of the poor vis-à-vis the FRBS.

Micro Finance- Indian Experience

There are no clear and systematic estimates available regarding the actual as well potential demand and supply of micro finance in the country. Regarding the estimation of target group for microfinance services, one can base it on the official estimation of the number of poor in the country as indicative of the total potential given the fact that micro-finance is meant for the poor. The estimated size of the Below Poverty Line (BPL) population gives some idea about the potential client base of the sector. Taking the official estimation of BPL population of 260 million during 1990-2000 and the average household size, we find that there are about 52.04 million households who are in the BPL category. The number of BPL households in rural areas comes to about 38.6 million; the same in urban areas comes to about 13.4 million. There are, however, arguments whether the entire BPL households should be considered for the purpose of providing microfinance. But given the fact that even very poor households need service like savings and insurance, if not credit always, one can safely consider almost all the households below poverty line (BPL) as potential client base of microfinance. Adjusting for changes like population growth and households crossing poverty line during the interval, one can say about 50 million households in the country presently constitute the basic target group of the micro-finance sector.

As regard the demand, based on the available estimates in the report of the Task Force of National Bank for Agricultural and Rural Development on microfinance it was indicated that the potential annual credit requirement could be in the range of Rs. 15,000 crore to Rs. 50,000 crores per year (NABARD 2000).[6] A recent un-official estimate puts the total credit demand by the poor households in the order of Rs.15, 000 to Rs. 45,000 crores households as reported in various studies and not the potential demand mainly base these estimates on the actual credit usage, which could be even higher. Due to variations in the average household credit use as estimated by different studies, there is a wide gap in the range of total estimated credit demand.

Since there are no clear figures available on the actual supply of microfinance, here we look at the level of lending and outreach of the target group attained by the major apex level microfinance institutions in the country. Table - 3.2 gives some macro level details about the lending and outreach performance of the major apex level microfinance institutions or schemes in the country based on 2007 and 2008 data. It is possible that there may be some overlaps in the coverage of these agencies as some of the Micro-Finance Institutions and NGOs may be simultaneously

Table - 3.2
Outreach of Microfinance Institutions in India

Apex Agencies	*No. of NGOs/ MFIs Involved*	*%*	*No. of SHGs (In Lakhs)*	*%*	*Outreach of Households (in Million)*	*%*	*Cumulative Loan Disbursement (Rs. In Million)*	*%*
NABARD's SHG-Bank Linkage (2004)	560	31.96	10.79	97.82	16.00	91.12	39,042	92.99
SFMC (2003)	169	9.65	-	0	0.91	5.18	1,181	2.83
RMK (2004)	749	42.75	0.24	2.18	0.48	2.73	1,034	2.46
FWWB (2003)	247	14.10	-	0	0.17	0.97	607	1.44
NABARD's RFA (2003)	27	1.54	-	0	-	0	120	0.28
Total	1752	100	11.03	100	17.55	100	41,984	100

Source: NABARD Report.

getting assistance from more than one agency. There may also be some NGOs or government sponsored microfinance programmes like SGSY, which may not be fully covered under these apex level programmes. Hence, one needs to take the figures in the Table only as indicative of the total actual outreach and supply.

In terms of the actual number of agencies or institutions involved at the grassroots or retail level, from Table - 3.2 one can make out that about 1752 institutions of different types were involved in delivering micro finance during 2007-2008. Under the SHG-Bank Linkage Programme of NABARD, about 560 financial institutions – Co-operatives, RRBs and Commercial Banks have participated across the country. Under the SHG-Bank Linkage Programme, the financial institutions have financed about 10.8 lakh SHGs which are promoted either directly by them or by the NGOs. NABARD provides refinance to these financial

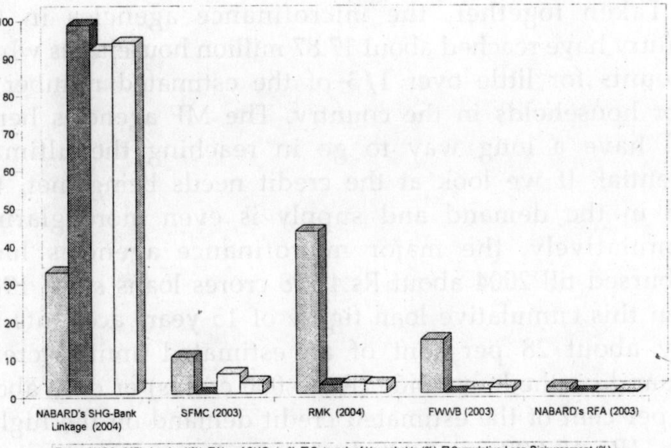

institutions for lending to SHGs. Besides these financial institutions, a large number of NGOs and microfinance institutions are also involved in delivering microfinance. About 1192 NGO/MFIs had received loan assistance from various apex institutions like SFMC, RMK, FWWB and NABARD for their on-lending programme. These 1192

NGOs/MFIs have approached the apex agencies for getting various types of loan assistance for on lending to their groups or members. Cumulatively, these NGOs/MFIs have reached out to over 1.56 million households and have received cumulatively about Rs. 2,942 million of loan assistance from apex agencies for lending. In addition to these 1192 NGO/ MFIs, it is estimated that another about 500 NGOs with an outreach of 0.32 million households are also involved in delivering microfinance in the country. These are mostly smaller NGOs which are managing their microfinance programmes either using donor funds or savings mobilized by their SHGs. Taking even these NGOs into account, one can say that as of 2007-2008, about 1700 NGOs/ MFIs are involved in delivering microfinance in the country apart from the 560 mainstreams financial institutions involved under the SHG-Bank Linkage Programme.

Taken together, the microfinance agencies in the country have reached about 17.87 million households which accounts for little over 1/3 of the estimated number of poor households in the country. The MF agencies hence still have a long way to go in reaching the ultimate potential. If we look at the credit needs being met, the gap in the demand and supply is even more glaring. Cumulatively, the major microfinance agencies have disbursed till 2004 about Rs.4,198 crores loans since 1989. Even this cumulative loan figure of 15 years accounts for only about 28 per cent of an estimated annual credit demand on the lower side (Rs.15,000 crores) or only about 9.3 per cent of the estimated credit demand on the higher side (Rs.45,000 crores). Instead of cumulative loan disbursement, if one were to take the actual annual loan disbursement of these agencies, then the gap would be even bigger. The gap probably could be even bigger if we were to take the total potential demand and not one based on the actual credit use.[7]

As regards savings and insurance, again there are no clear macro level statistics available. But going by the fact that the micro finance agencies in the country so far have focused their attention mainly on credit, and also that many local micro finance institutions are not able to mobilize savings in a full fledged way due to legal restrictions, the extent of gap in the demand and supply for these services would be definitely much higher than the credit. Thus, given the need and their current level of achievements, the MFIs and other agencies have still a long way to go in meeting the needs of the poor.[8]

It is true "that some of the states, particularly in the north, east and northeastern regions, have a cheerer history of dealing with formal credit. It, therefore, calls for significant preparatory work to put an alternative credit mechanism in place that would benefit these regions. This process of capability building and social mobilization cannot be accelerated. It may be noted that the success of the SHG-bank linkage programme in states like Andhra Pradesh is attributed to the existence of strong institutions involved in social intermediation, which help in the formation of SHG's". (M.S.Shriram: 2005:pp.1702). [9]

The present SGSY scheme is a revamped form of the earlier IRDP launched in 1999. The latter's drawbacks were removed in the new scheme. SHG's are used to disburse a part of loan to the rural poor. The SHG model is expected to help in beneficiary identification through participatory methods. The subsidy element is back-ended in order for it to work as an incentive to pay back the loans. The rates of subsidy have also been rationalized. Under this programme, a sum of Rs.1109 crore of bank credit was disbursed for about 8 lakh poor people in 2001-02 of which the share of women is 40 percent.'

It is found that NGO's or NGO-MFI's play a major role in the micro finance sector in India, but these are largely unregulated. Some are partially regulated to the extent that they have sought grants from foreign sources and file annual returns with the union home ministry. The only regulated institutions in this sector are the few NBFC's.

Table – 3.3
Growth of SHG-Bank Linkage Programme

Year	*No.of groups*	*Growth Rate*	*Amount of loan (Rs.Million)*	*Growth Rate*
1999-00	255	-	2.83	-
2000-01	620	143.133	6.53	130.74
2001-02	2122	242.25	24.45	274.42
2002-03	4757	124.1753	60.58	147.77
2003-04	8598	80.74	228.36	276.95
2004-05	14317	66.51	237.95	4.19
2005-06	32995	130.46	520.60	118.78
2006-07	114775	247.85	1501.26	188.37
2007-08	234843	104.61	4007.46	166.93
Average		142.46		163.52

Source: NABARD documents.

The formal financial agencies were not lending to the rural low-income groups and the rural poor till mid 1990's. To fill these gaps the SHG's were set up with SGO's acting as facilitators or intermediaries. The NABARD pilot project in Karnataka (1986-87) was a beginning in the direction of linking SHG's with formal financial agencies like banks, mediating through NGO's. This project known as the SHG-bank linkage programme was advantageous to the commercial banks in view of their responsibility to fulfill their social goals like helping the poor and achieving operational efficiency (by externalizing part of their transaction cost). During 1999-00, only 255 SHG's were linked to banks with Rs.2.89 million as refinance facility from NABARD. But by 2007-08, SHG-Bank linkage was rapidly expanded linking 2,34,843 SHG's with a refinance

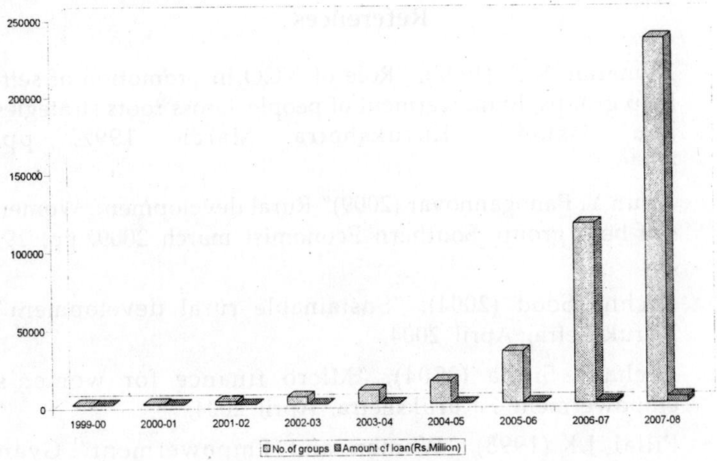

of Rs.4,007.46 million. This scheme is expended to 412 districts of 25 states and two UT's in India.

Summary

The SHG – Bank Linkage Programme has been heralded as one of the largest microfinance programmes in the World. The SHG movement involves common people across the country with their main strength being mutual interest, informality and flexibility. It is, therefore, desirable that their organisational structure, method of raising funds, interest rate, and structure should be left to themselves. The interference with the design of the SHG movement has the potential to vitiate the credit culture and affect the relationship of SHGs with the banking structure. But steps to consolidate the movement and upgrade their activities from intra-lending to income-generating activities, and group microenterprises are welcome development, which the banking sector should encourage and support as part of social banking. Lastly, the MFIs hold significant potential for reaching the financial services to the poor people provided it can address the critical challenges confronting them such as sustainability, capital, capacity and transparency.

References

1. Kumaran. K.P. (1997), "Role of NGO in promotion of self-help groups, Empowerment of people: Gross roots strategies and Issues", Kurukshetra March 1997, pp. 40-46.
2. Arjun Y. Panogannovar (2009)" Rural development; Women self-help group, Southern Economist march 2009, pp, 19-20.
3. Archna Sood (2004), "Sustainable rural development" Kurukshetra, April 2004.
4. Archana Sinha (2004), "Micro finance for women's empowerment", Kurukshetra, April 2004.
5. Pillai J.K.(1995) "Women and Empowerment" Gyan Publishing House, New Delhi, 1995.
6. Marilee Karl (1995) "Women's economic empowerment in south Asia, vaster publications New, Delhi, 1996, pp. 191-292.
7. Gurumurthy T.R.(2000), Self-help groups empower rural women Kurukshetra vol 48, No.5.
8. Murugan K.R and B.Dharmalingam (2000), Self-help groups new women's movement", social welfare, vol. 47, No.5, August 2000.
9. Sriraman. V.P. (2006), "Micro Finance, Self-help groups and Women Empowerment current issues and concerns", working paper 38.

4

National Policy for the Empowerment of Women (2001)

Introduction

This chapter gives an overview about 2001 national policy for the empowerment of women and it also includes goals and objectives of the policy and finally impact of the policy on women has been analysed.

The principle of gender equality is enshrined in the Indian Constitution in its Preamble, Fundamental Rights, Fundamental Duties and Directive Principles. The Constitution not only grants equality to women, but also empowers the State to adopt measures of positive discrimination in favour of women.

Within the framework of a democratic polity, our laws, development policies, plans and programmes have aimed at women's advancement in different spheres. From the Fifth Five Year Plan (1974 – 78) onwards has been a marked shift in the approach to women's issues from welfare to development. In recent years, the empowerment of women has been National Commission for Women was set up by an Act of Parliament in 74th Amendments (1993) to the Constitution of India have provided for reservation of seats in the local bodies of Panchayats and Municipalities for women, laying a strong foundation for their participation n decision making at the local levels.

India has also ratified various international conventions and human rights instruments committing to secure equal rights of women. Key among them is the ratification of the Convention on Elimination of All Forms of Discrimination Against Women (CEDAW) in 1993.

The Mexico Plan of Action (1975), the Nairobi Forward Looking Strategies (1985), the Beijing Declaration as well as the Platform for Action (1995) and the Outcome Document adopted by the UNDP session on Gender Equality and Development and Peace for the 21st Century, titled "Further actions and initiatives to implement the Beijing Declaration and the Platform for Action" have been unreservedly endorsed by India for appropriate follow up.

The Policy also takes note of the commitments of the Ninth Five year plan and the other Sectoral Policies relating to empowerment of women.

The women's movement and a widespread network of non - Government Organizations which have strong grass - roots presence and deep insight into women's concerns have contributed in inspiring initiatives for the empowerment of women.

However, there still exists a wide gap between the goals enunciated in the Constitution, legislation, policies, plans, programmes, and related mechanisms on the one hand and the situational reality of the status of women in India, on the other. This has been analyzed extensively in the However, there still exists a wide gap between the goals enunciated in the Constitution, legislation, policies, plans, programmes, and related mechanisms on the one hand and the situational reality of the status of women in India, on the other. This has been analyzed extensively in the Report of the Committee on the Status of Women in India, "Towards Equality", (1974) and highlighted in the National Perspective Plan for Women, 1998 - 2000, the Shramashakti Report, 1998 and the Platform for Action, Five years After - An assessment".

Gender disparity manifests itself in various forms, the most obvious being the trend of continuously declining female ration in the population in the last few decades. Social stereotyping and violence at the domestic and societal levels are some of the other manifestations. Discrimination against girl children, adolescent girls and women persists in parts of the country.

The underlying causes of gender inequality are related to social and economic structure, which is based on informal and formal norms and practices.

Consequently, the access of women particularly those belonging to weaker sections including Scheduled Casts /Scheduled Tribes/ Other Backward Classes and minorities, majority of whom are in the rural areas and in the informal, unorganized sector - to education, health and productive resources, among others, in inadequate. Therefore, they remain largely marginalized, poor and socially excluded.

Goal and objectives

The goal of this policy is to bring about the advancement, development and empowerment of women. The Policy will be widely disseminated so as to encourage active participation of all stakeholders for achieving its goals. Specially, the objectives of this Policy include.

(i) Creating an environment through positive economic and social policies for full development of women to enable them to realize their full potential.

(ii) The de - jure and de - facto enjoyment of all human rights and fundamental freedom by women on equal basis with men in all spheres - political, economics, social, cultural and civil.

(iii) Equal access to participation and decision making

of women in social, political and economic life of the nation.

(iv) Equal access to women to health care, quality education at all levels, career and vocational guidance, employment, equal remuneration, occupational health and safety, social security and public office etc.

(v) Strengthening legal systems aimed at elimination of all forms of discrimination against women.

(vi) Changing societal attitudes and community practices by active participation and involvement of both men and women.

(vii) Mainstreaming a gender perspective in the development process.

(viii) Elimination of discrimination and all forms of violence against women and the girl child ; and

(ix) Building and strengthening partnerships with civil society, particularly women's organizations.

Policy Prescription

Legal - Judicial system will be made more responsive and gender sensitive to women's needs, especially in cases of domestic violence and personal assault. New laws will be enacted and existing laws reviewed to ensure that justice is quick and the punishment meted out to the culprits is commensurate with the severity of the offence.

At the Institute of and with the full participation of all stakeholders including community and religious leaders, the Policy would aim to encourage changes in personal laws such as those related to marriage, divorce, maintenance and guardianship so as to eliminate discrimination against women. The evolution of property rights in a patriarchal system has contributed to the subordinate status of women. The Policy would aim to encourage changes in laws relating to ownership of property and inheritance by evolving consensus in order to make them gender justice.

Decision Making

Women's equality in power sharing and active participation in decision making, including decision making in political process at all levels will be ensured for the achievement of the goals of empowerment. All measures will be taken to guarantee women equal access to and full participation in decision making bodies at every level, including the legislative, executive, judicial, corporate, statutory bodies, as also the advisory Commissions, Committees, Boards, Trusts etc. Affirmative action such as reservations/quotas, including in higher legislative bodies, will be considered whenever necessary on a time bound basis. Women - friendly personnel policies will also be drawn up to encourage women to participate effectively in the developmental process.

Mainstreaming a Gender Perspective in the Development Process

Policies, programmes and systems will be established to ensure mainstreaming of women's perspectives in all developmental processes, as catalysts, participants and recipients. Whereever there are gaps in policies and programmes, women specific interventions would be undertaken to bridge these. Coordinating and monitoring mechanisms will also be devised to assess from time to time the progress of such mainstreaming mechanisms. Women's issues and concerns as a result will specially be addresses and reflected in all concerned laws, sectoral policies, plans and programmes of action.

Economic Empowerment of Women

Since women comprise the majority of the population below the poverty line and are very often in situations of extreme poverty, given the harsh realities of intra - household and social discrimination, macro economic policies and poverty eradication programmes will specially address the needs and problems of such women. There will be improved implementation of programmes which are already women oriented with special targets for women. Steps will be taken for mobilization of poor women and convergence of services, by offering them a range of economic and social options, along with necessary support measures to enhance their capabilities.

Women poverty is increasing throughout the region and that the manifestations of the impact of globalization continue to be felt. The working group identified a number of policies that aggravate and contribute to the feminization of poverty. These include privatization and corporationisation of knowledge and resources as well as public services, trade liberalization, deregulation of economics, withdrawal of subsidies, downsizing of Government, substitution of food production by cash crops and the inflow of foreign capital and enterprise. The working group indicated these measures have lead to unemployment, underemployment, retrenchment and the shift to labour form formal to informal sector and regular to unprotected, subcontracted labour of women workers.

Ferminization of poverty increases with the increase in poverty. The international trade region has increased the gap between the rich and poor countries and the rich and poor within the countries[1] .

National and international institutions must develop the holistic definition of poverty so that comparisons overtime and across regimes can be made. Fundamental institutions and other credit institutions must provide break through credits to women for increasing their income on a continuous basis. Poverty eradication programmes must address gender inequalities within and outside the households. Government must enact laws to protect equal property rights to women.

Micro Credit

In order to enhance women's access to credit for consumption and production, the establishment of new, and strengthening of existing micro - credit mechanisms and micro - finance institution will be undertaken so that the outreach of credit is enhanced. Other supportive measures would be taken to ensure adequate flow of credit through extent financial institutions and banks, so that all women below poverty line have easy access to credit.

Economic participation of the women is continued to struggle to access finance and other economic resources at both micro and macro levels. At the income that they now largely generate from their own labour. At the macro level prevailing business practices continued to marginalize women's enterprises and small businesses from sources of capital and information. The access of low income in particular to capital, credit and technology remains poor despite the claimed successes of micro credit programmes. Provisions for social security benefits for women workers remain inadequate in many countries.

Re - examine the impact of micro credit and income generating programmes genuinely empowering women economically and socially. Rapidly expand the provision of credit and capital to the poor women and provide supporting infrastructure. Work for the creation economic platforms where women will have control of financial resources, to enhances their empowerment.

Globalisation

Globalization has presented new challenges for the realization of the goal of women's equality, the gender impact of which has not been systematically evaluated fully. However, from the micro - level studies that were commissioned by the Department of Women & Child Development, it is evident that there is a need for re - framing policies for access to employment and quality of employment. Benefits of the growing global economy have been unevenly distributed leading to wider economic disparities, the feminization of poverty, increased gender inequality through often deteriorating working conditions and unsafe working environment especially in the informal economy and rural areas. Strategies will be design to enhance the capacity of women and empower them to meet the negative social and economic impacts, which may flow from the globalization process.

The impact of globalization and economic restructuring resulting in increased workloads for women, including low paid and unpaid work as well as reductions in social security provisions Government and corporations should provide adequate facility and support mechanisms to harmonize work and family responsibilities for women. Government should measure and value unpaid work with a system of coordination between the national machinery and the statistics division. Government to improve statistics, which underestimate women's unemployment as under employment.

Women and Industry

The important role - played by women in electronics, information technology and food processing and agro industry and textiles has been crucial to the development of these sectors. They would be given comprehensive support in terms of labour legislation, social security and other support services to participate in various industrial sectors.

Women at present cannot work in night shift in factories even if they wish to. Suitable measures will be taken to enable women to work on the night shift in factories. This will be accompanied with support services for security, transportation etc.

Support Services

The provision of support services for women, like child care facilities, including creches at work places and educational institutions, homes for the aged and the disabled will be expanded and improved to create an enabling environment and to ensure their full cooperation in social, political and economic life. Women - friendly personnel policies will also be drawn up to encourage women to participate effectively in the developmental process.

Strategies for Economic Empowerment

1. Women are beginning to obtain training skills and be in professions, which are non – traditional, and thus they penetrate the so - called 'male' domain.
2. Organizing of women on the basis of work is crucial.
3. Strategies must address needs and concerns into development structures must be created for both.
4. Organizations, which are based on charity or male dominated membership, are most likely to become economically empowered.
5. Women's empowerment in the region must be ecologically sensitive, This must be integrated into all strategies.
6. Women's empowerment must not restrict itself to income, generating processes but include other components such as capacity building, control over production, tools and process, conservation of natural resources, strengthening people's organizations and social security.
7. Training processes should be processes of collective learning and empowerment.
8. Training centers have and should establish a link for recruitment of trainees with the relevant job markets.
9. The market should be studied and surveyed adequately before production is undertaken on a large scale.
10. Marketing strategies devised and undertaken suggest that.
    a. The NGO staff themselves should do advertising.
    b. Diversity products – leaving a diverse product and price range.

c. Develop a theme for the consumers as part of the marketing strategy for example ; it could be something that can develop the pride in weaving hand made clothes.
d. Extensive participation in trade fairs.
e. Develop an outside market but first tap the local market completely.
f. NGOs exporting the products should interface with NGOs in the importing countries both for market information and lobbying with consumers.
g. Women's groups and NGOs should themselves be self sufficient, and generate their own funds - rather than basing their economic empowerment work on grants and subsidies.
h. Devising organizational structures, which allow for government bodies to be accountable to poor women, and for women to have a dialogue with governments, can and have become a strategy for economic empowerment.

Women and Economy

Women's perspectives will be included in designing and implementing macro - economic and social policies by institutionalizing their participation in such processes. Their contribution to socio - economic development as producers and workers will be recognized in the formal and informal sectors (including home based workers) and appropriate policies relating to employment.

Expected Outcome

The participants will understand the contribution of women in the work and will acquire knowledge about the invisibilities of women's contribution in and its reasons. They also discuss exploitation of women on the field of work and strategies to improve participation of women in economy and to make visible.

Invisibilities of Women's Contribution on Economy

Women share double burden as the producers of human race as well as supporters and sustainers of the human life. They make up one third of the workforce but their contributions on economy remains invisible. Most of the women in India are engaged in household or domestic work, which constitute a vital but grossly undervalued type of economic activity. Domestic work does not quality as productive activity as per the census of India definition. Working women, as per the census definition are those who are domestic as well other works. There is gross under reporting of contribution of women in work in the official statistics. Direct and Indirect contribution of women to the household is enormous. The data under estimate their contribution to family income. Women are engaged in several activities which add to how should income but are totally outside the sphere of the market economy besides there. Most of the women and girls do most of the house hold unpaid work. For example, collection of fuel and water, looking after children and animals kitchen gardening, food processing, sewing and weaving etc.

Characteristics of Female Workers

Women are marginalized in the world of work due to several socio - cultural reasons; most of the female worker is a marginal worker having worked for less than 183 days over the 12 months. According to 1991 census 86 percent women workers are marginal workers among women is several times higher than men. There is a great difference in work force participation of women in rural and urban areas. Women are legally engaged in low paid primary sector. Female workers have limited occupation choices. Nearly 80 percent of women workers are engaged in agricultural activities mainly as agricultural laborers.

The secondary and the tertiary sector account for only 80.9 percent and 90.5 percent respective of the total female workers in secondary and tertiary sectors, they are confined to home based service industries and law paid traditional an d semi skilled occupations. Almost 90 - 94 percent of women workers are engaged in unorganized and informal sectors. Female work force participation is declining due to introduction of new technologies.

Exploitation of Women in the World of Work

Economic development has marginalized women and women have to overwork than the stipulated hours. Women are victims of centuplication and intermittence of work. Sometimes they are underpaid and there is discrimination between wages of men and women .There is an increase in the incidence of female child labour. A large number of them are engaged in gem polishing, beedi rolling and other hazardous occupations. Constitutional and legal provisions are needed for equal participation of women in economy.

Strategies to improve women's participation in economy; make women's work visible and provide more work opportunities for women to educate them. Women to be sensitized about their rights demand the same and fight against the oppressed. Identify small organization at illegal levels and strengthen by providing necessary technical and vocational training to women, especially to rural women.

Preparing women for action, educational, social, economic and political. The participants will develop skills preparing women for Educational, Social, Economic and Political actions.

Need to prepare women for individual and collective action in the areas of social, political and economic issues - despite the fact that government has passed so many laws to help women and more and more women are working in different fields, problems of girls and women are there.

Prepare women according to the needs – Problems of girls / women differ from region to region and in different age groups. Therefore, action required will be of different nature.

For Educational Action – Develop Skills in Women

1. For organizing awareness campaigns.
2. For effective group functioning and group leadership.
3. Efficient communication skills in relation to illiterate and deprived groups.
4. Collection of data and household information.
5. To identify needs of community.

Generate Awareness among women about

1. Socio - Cultural impediments to literacy.
2. Forces in society and causes of oppression and marginalization in case of women.
3. National literacy mission.
4. Non - formal Education .
5. Incentives for SC and ST girls and girls of other background communities and women.
6. Pre - school education.
7. Adult education and income generating scheme.

For Social Action

- Mobilizing women
- Strategies should be chosen for changing values, attitudes and behavior.
- Awareness about government schemes / programmes and other organizations for up - liftment of women and helping women in distress.
- Awareness of mass media as a tool for spreading messages.
- Influencing society and family as tools for improving position of women.

For Economic Action

- Awareness about land, water, fores, distribution patterns and issues of injustice for women.
- Identification of raw materials, which can be exploited for employment.
- Information about employment opportunity existing government schemes/programmes for helping women economically.
- Opportunities for income generation - technical information and feasibility, government's income generating schemes.
- Knowledge of marketing.
- Awareness of local economic institution, banks and co-operatives.

Women and Economy

- Land water and forest distribution pattern and issues of injustice.
- Women and occupation - Identification of raw materials, which can be explored for employment.
- Poultry, Piggery, sheep rearing, Dairy, Sericulture etc.
- Opportunities for income generation, technical information and feasibility.
- Unpaid labour inputs by women.
- Women and marketing. Access lack of cheating by middlemen and other problems.
- Local crops and improves methods of storage.
- Local Economic Institutions and Women's role in it Cooperatives Banks Cooperative laws.
- Family budget and income management and women's role in it.

References

1. Ghosh, Jayati (1996). 'Macroeconomic Treads and Female Employment in India in the Asian Context', Paper Presented

at the Seminar on Gender and Employment in India: Recent Trends, Patterns and Policy Options, Organized by The Indian Society for Labour Economics and Institute of Economic Growth, New Delhi, Dec- 18 - 30.

2. Gurumoorthy. T.R. (2002): Economic Empowerment Through Self - -Reliance. Social Welfare, Delhi.
3. Gurumoorthy. T.R. (2002): Economic Empowerment Through Self - -Reliance. Social Welfare, Delhi.
4. Hashemi, Syed M., Sidney Ruth Schuler, and Ann P. Riley. 1996. "Rural credit programs and women's empowerment in Bangladesh." World Development 24(4): 635-653.
5. Kaladhar.K (1997) Microfinance in India - Design, Structure and Governance. Economic and Political Weekly, Oct 18 : 2687-2706.
6. Kalpagam, U. (1999), 'Women, Work and Domestic Duties: Income Planning for Housewives", The Indian Journal of Labour Economics, Vol. 42, No.2, October - December 1999, PP.567 - 580.
7. Karmakar K.G(1999) rural credit and self-help groups; Micro Finance needs and concepts in India sage publication, New Delhi.
8. Karmakar,K.G(1999) Rural Credit and Self Help Groups - Microfinance Needs and Concepts in India. New Delhi: Sage Publications.

5

SHGs and Micro Finance Programmes in Karnataka

Introduction

This chapter highlights the current status of micro finance sector in the state of Karnataka in terms of potential demand for micro finance services, current level of outreach and supply in relation to the potential, and extent of involvement of various types of institutions. The rural bankers, SHGs and some government functionaries have done splendid work in the development of self-help groups in the state of Karnataka. The state of Karnataka has been a pioneer in the programme of SHG Bank linkage and is indeed hailed as a laboratory for micro finance innovations. Ubder the "Stree Shakhi" programme of government of Karnataka, the Department of Women and Child Welfare is actively involved in the promotion of SHGs. On the other hand the Regina l Rural Banks have themselves promoted tens of thousands of SHGs and have credit linked them a commendable service indeed.

Micro- Finance or Micro-Credit for the poor and women has received extensive recognition as a strategy for poverty reduction and for economic empowerment. Increasingly in the last five years, there is a questioning of whether micro-credit is the most effective approach to economic empowerment of the poorest and, among them, women in particular. Development practitioners in India and developing countries often argue that the exaggerated focus on micro-credit as a solution for the poor has led to neglect by the state and public institutions in addressing employment and livelihood needs of the poor. With the onset of structural adjustment programmes in the early nineties, there was a public debate around reduced state spending on social sectors. In a country like India, economic uncertainties, loss of livelihood, inflation, lack of access to natural resources, declining employment, increasing social unrest, natural disaster, etc., make the poor extremely vulnerable. In this context it would be necessary to ensure that the poor are empowered to access development resources and use it to their greatest benefit. [1]

Equitable gains from development on a sustainable basis and ensuring viability of financial services are the key elements in a strategy of poverty reduction by means of credit support to the poor. As micro-finance is seen to be an approach addressing these concerns effectively; it has assumed significance in all the developing countries as an effective tool in fighting poverty.

Micro- Finance includes savings, credit, insurance and other financial institutions and policy makers prefer not to make any distinction. Credit for empowerment is about organizing people, particularly around credit and building capacities to manage money. The focus is on getting the poor to mobilize their own funds, building their capacities and empowering them to leverage external credit. Perception of women is that learning to manage money and rotate funds builds women's capacities and confidence to intervene in local development and local governance beyond the limited goals of ensuring access to credit. Further, it combines the goals of financial sustainability with that of creating community owned institutions. [2]

Before 1990s credit schemes for rural women were almost negligible. The concept of women's credit was born on the insistence by women oriented studies that highlighted the discrimination and struggle of women in having access to credit. However, there is a perceptible gap in financing genuine credit needs of the poor especially women in the rural sector.

There are certain misconceptions about the poor people that they need loan at subsidized rates of interest on soft terms, they lack education, skills, capacity to save, credit worthiness and therefore are not bankable. Nevertheless, the experience of several SHGs that rural poor is actually efficient managers of credit and finance. Availability of timely and adequate credit is essential for them to undertake any economic activity rather than credit subsidy. [3]

The government measures have attempted to help the poor by implementing different poverty alleviation programmes but with little success. Since most of them are target based involving lengthy procedures for loan disbursements, high transaction costs, and lack of supervision and monitoring. Since the credit requirements of the rural poor cannot be adopted on project lending approach as it is in the case of organized sector, there emerged the need for an informal credit supply through SHGs. The rural poor with the assistance from NGOs have demonstrated their potential for self help to secure economic and financial strength. Various case studies show that there is a positive correlation between credit availability and women's empowerment.

Micro finance has rightly gained he support of financial institutions, policy makers and NGOs, the world over, as an effective means for ameliorating living conditions of the poor. Many experiments have been made in different countries to reach out to the have-nots and to extend credit support to them. However, the poorest segments of he rural economy still remain outside their reach. They have certainly a long way to go to attain he desirable goal of reaching them and elevating their living conditions. It requires the combined efforts of a number of agencies to help them by holding their hands and escorting them on the exalted road to self-reliance. Hurdles on the road are too many. But they are not insurmountable, given the determination to reach out to them. [4]

Self-Help Groups have emerged as a collective, informal agency for encouraging thrift and for obtaining micro-finance. Over 20 lakh SHGs are in existence in India today, providing the basic grass root-level institutional support to over 2.4 crore households. Banks, supported by NABARD, and NGOs attracted by the scope available for empowering the poor, are behind the show. There is a proliferation of the number of members joining SHG movement. Time-bound targets are being fixed to expand their base. Mere quantitative expansion is not sufficient to lift them above the poverty line. After they are raised above that ubiquitous line with credit facilities, it is necessary to support them at least for some time, so that they do not slip down, back into the unhappy situation.

Considering the enormity of the work involved in reaching out to all the households, a multi-agency approach is inevitable. Besides banks, NGOs and micro-finance institutions also have specific roles to play in this task. Micro finance institutions sponsored by NGOs and others are expected to be active players in this field, operating in different areas depending up on their suitability and acceptability. [5]

Micro-Finance Experience in Karnataka

The Karnataka State is situated between 11. 31^{0} and

18. 45^0 north latitudes and 74 .12′ and 78.40′ east longitudes and lies in the west-central part of peninsular India. Its maximum length from north to south is about 700km and from east to west 400 km. It is bound on the north by Maharashtra State, on the north - west by Goa, on the east by Andhra Pradesh, on the south and south - east by Tamilnadu, on south - west by Kerala and on the west by Arabian Sea.

Area and population

Karnataka State covers an area of 1,91,791 sq km or occupies 5.35 percent of the total geographical area of the country. The growth of population in absolute terms it has been increased from 370 lakhs in 1981, 449 lakhs in 1991 and 527 lakhs in 2001. The male population is also increased in absolute terms from 188 percent to 268 percent 1.58 per annum and in case of female population; its growth rate also declined from 1.91 percent to 1.61 percent. The growth rate in female is higher than that of male in two decades.

Literacy

During 1991 the literacy rate was 56.00 percent and it has increased to 67 percent in 2001. The literacy of rural male has increased from 60.3 percent to 70.6 percent. Female rate has also increased to 34.8 percent to 48.5 percent.

SC and ST Population

A vast majority of people belonging to the Scheduled Castes and Scheduled Tribes in Karnataka live in rural areas. According to 2001 census the Scheduled Castes and Scheduled Tribes account for 16.2 percent and 6.6 percent of the total population of the State, respectively, whereas in India the proportion of these two constitute 16.2 percent and 8.2 percent respectively. . The percentage of both categories have increased by 1.5 percent and 2.3 percent respectively during 1991 and 2001.

Standard of Living

In Karnataka, while major part of the income of the people is spent on daily necessities of life such as food, clothing, shelter, etc., expenditure on education, medical care and other durable goods is not significant. However, there are occasions when the families have to spend a large amount on social and religious ceremonies and those causing indebtedness. States like Punjab, Haryana, Maharashtra and Tamilnadu have a better standard of living than Karnataka.

Agriculture and Irrigation

Karnataka, like India, had depended mainly on agriculture in ancient times. Even in the pre-historic times, cereals like ragi, wheat, paddy and huruli were grown in Karnataka as charred remains of these grains have been found in many pre-historic sites. People in ancient Karnataka realized the importance of agriculture. Inscriptions divide agricultural land as Gadde or wet land, Charade or land depending only on rain and beddalu or dry land. Rice was the main crop in wet lands and manasollasa speaks of eight varieties of rice, which include Gandhashali or perfumed rice, Raktashali or red rice and Sookshmashali small rice, what is called sannakki.

SHG-Bank Linkage Programme in Karnataka

Banking institutions in Karnataka as promoting agencies of SHGs lent micro credit for different activities. The details of micro credit lent by banks in Karnataka are presented in the Table- 5.1

Table- 5.1
Micro-Credit lent by Banks in Karnataka (upto 2008)

Sl. No	District	SHGs financed (Number)	Ratio	Amount Len (Rs.t in crore)	Ratio
01	Bagalkote	2,803	1.25	11.47	1.16
02	Bangalore Rural	8,030	3.57	53.21	5.38
03	Bangalore Urban	3,083	1.37	18.81	1.90
04	Belgaum	9,675	4.30	47.80	4.83
05	Bellary	9,796	4.35	37.71	3.81
06	Bidar	10,449	4.64	51.86	5.24
07	Bijapur	5,760	2.56	19.40	1.96
08	Chamarajanagar	5,889	2.62	25.86	2.62
09	Chikamagalur	3,736	1.66	16.37	1.66
10	Chitradurga	8,717	3.87	34.65	3.50
11	Dakshina Kannada	23,901	10.62	76.29	7.71
12	Davanagere	6,268	2.79	32.22	3.26
13	Dharwad5	,134	2.28	21.83	2.21
14	Gadag	3,308	1.47	14.12	1.43
15	Gulbarga	12,279	5.46	43.06	4.35
16	Hassan	17,374	7.72	78.91	7.98
17	Haveri	4,797	2.13	23.98	2.42
18	Kodagu	3,296	1.47	12.63	1.28
19	Kolar	9,669	4.30	42.47	4.29
20	Koppal	3,296	1.47	12.63	1.28
21	Mandya	10,275	4.57	44.17	4.47
22	Mysore	15,043	6.69	69.90	7.07
23	Raichur	4,550	2.02	16.63	1.68
24	Shimoga	7,215	3.21	31.57	3.19
25	Tumkur	14,682	6.53	76.55	7.74
26	Udupi	10,042	4.46	46.04	4.66
27	Uttara Kannada	5,907	2.63	28.76	2.91
	State Total	2,24,974	100	988.90	100

Source: NABARD Reports.

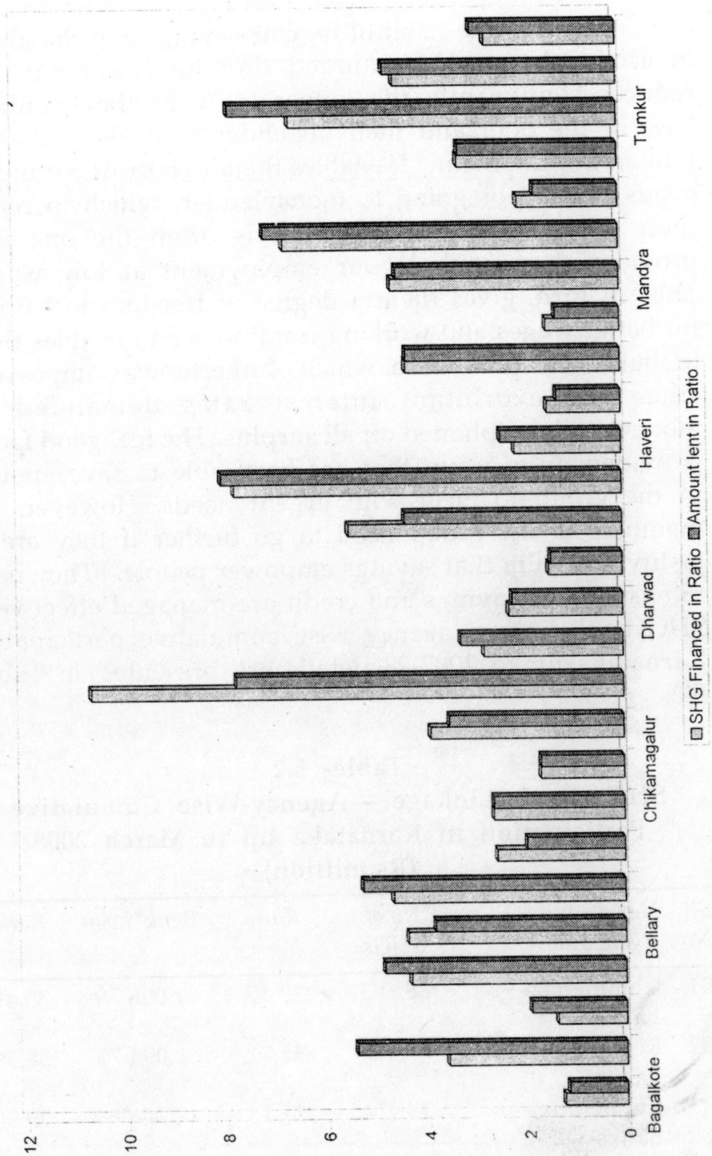
12
10
8
6
4
2
0
Bagalkote
Bellary
Chikamagalur
Dharwad
Haveri
Mandya
Tumkur
SHG Financed in Ratio
Amount lent in Ratio

The livelihood needs of the poor - The income and basic needs perspective of poverty:

Cultivating the habit of regular savings and the ability to access them when required through credit not only reduces significantly the vulnerability of the livelihood base of the poor and their dependence, it also enhances human development.[6] It enables them to borrow for urgent needs instead of going to moneylender, which increases their dependency since he/she is often the one who provides them with labour employment at low wages. This, in turn, gives them a degree of freedom to bargain for better wages and working conditions and enables them to build a capital base which, hitherto was impossible since the exorbitant interest rates demanded by moneylenders siphoned off all surplus. The feel good factor is evident in a group that has been able to save enough in the group to meet with urgent needs. However, the members of the group need to go further if they are to justify the claim that savings empower people.[7] They need to ensure that savings and credit are managed effectively. SHG bank linkage agency wise cumulative participation Karnataka up to 2007-08 details are presented in Table-5.2.

Table- 5.2
SHG- Bank Linkage - Agency-Wise Cumulative Participation in Karnataka up to March 2008 (Rs.million)

Sl. No	*Name of the Agency*	*No.of SHGs*	*Ratio*	*Bank Loan*	*Ratio*
01	Commercial Banks	38,605	37.17	1,006.79	35.49
02	Regional Rural Banks	37,087	35.71	1,094.73	38.59
03	Cooperative Banks	28,174	27.13	734.66	25.90
	Total	103,866	100	2,836.18	100

Source: NABARD Report.

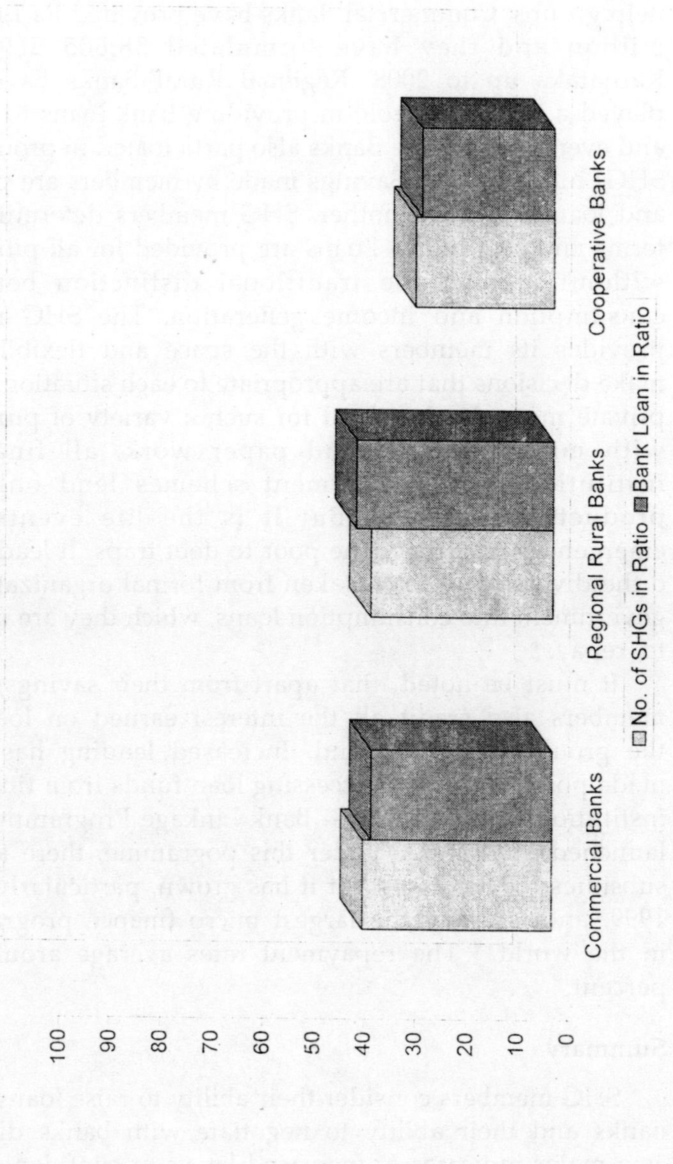
100
90
80
70
60
50
40
30
20
10
0
Commercial Banks
Regional Rural Banks
Cooperative Banks
No. of SHGs in Ratio
Bank Loan in Ratio

The above table clearly shows that all the financial institutions have provided maximum bank loan to self-help groups. Commercial Banks have provided Rs.1,006.79 million and they have formulated 38,605 SHGs in Karnataka up to 2008. Regional Rural Banks have also played a significant role in providing bank loans to SHGs and even Cooperative Banks also participated in promoting SHGs in Karnataka. Savings made by members are pooled and loaned to one another. SHG members determine the terms and conditions. Loans are provided for all purposes without making the traditional distinction between consumption and income generation. The SHG model provides its members with the space and flexibility to make decisions that are appropriate to each situation. Only private moneylenders lend for such a variety of purposes with minimum pass and paper work; all financial institutions and government schemes lend only for productive purposes. But it is the life events and emergencies that drive the poor to debt traps. It leads also o the diversion of loans taken from formal organizations/ government into consumption loans, which they are unable to repay. [8]

It must be noted, that apart from their savings, SHG members also credit all the interest earned on loans to the group's common fund. Increased lending has been made possible through accessing loan funds from financial institutions, after the SHG- Bank Linkage Programme was launched in 1991-92. Under this pogramme, there are no subsidies for the asset, yet it has grown, particularly after 1999, and is today the largest micro finance programme in the world. [9] The repayment rates average around 95 percent.

Summary

SHG members consider their ability to raise loans from banks and their ability to negotiate with banks directly as a major indicator of increased levels of confidence and self esteem. This provides some insights into SHG members

Table- 5.3

SHG- Bank Linkage – Physical & Financial Progress of Participating Regional Rural Banks upto 2007-08 (Rs. Million)

Name of the RRB	*Cumulative No of SHGs provided with bank loan upto 2007*	*No.of SHGs provided with bank loan during 2007-08*	*Cumulative bank loan disbursed upto 2007*	*Bank loan disbursed during 2007-08*	*Cumulative bank loan disbursed upto 2008*
Bijapur Grameena Bank	824	584	25.47	25.73	51.20
Cauvery Grameena Bank	4,114	2,087	119.81	81.56	201.37
Chikmagalur – Kodagu Grameena Bank	120	136	3.84	4.58	8.42
Chitradurga Grameena Bank	3,248	1,369	95.63	46.50	142.13
Kalpatharu Grameena Bank	1,612	1,875	38.96	75.05	114.01
Kolar Grameena Bank	1,203	865	31.42	22.23	53.65
Krishna Grameena Bank	2,409	1,579	70.32	35.84	106.16
Malaprabha Grameena Bank	2,557	2,981	55.33	88.70	144.03
Netravati Grameena Bank	747	194	20.99	5.90	26.89
Sahyadri Grameena Bank	1,420	332	55.04	26.10	81.14
Tungabhadra Grameena Bank	3,152	2,410	76.55	47.84	124.39
Varada Grameena Bank	219	271	4.51	9.84	14.35
Visveswaraya Grameena Bank	304	475	6.96	20.03	26.99
Total	21,929	15,158	604.83	489.90	1,094.73

Source: NABARD Report.

ability to access finance from mainstream institutions. Many members say that the learnt to sign after joining the group. Although this might seem like a minor achievement to most of us., to SHG members, it seems to be away of gaining acceptance in the 'mainstream' and a source of pride. Many members spoke of how they were previously ashamed to conduct bank transactions, as they used thumb impressions in place of signatures. Only after learning to sign were they comfortable about going to a bank. It was after joining the SHG, that the had gained the confidence of conducting bank transactions on their own, and approaching bank officials for loans.

References

1. Ariz Ahmed M (1999), "Women Empowerment Self Help Groups", Kurukshethra, April, 47, 7-19-20 and 49.
2. Chirangee T (2003), Empowering Women Through Self Help Groups Experiences in Experiment", Kurukshetra, March.
3. Dodkey M.D (1999), " SHG and Micro Credit Sustaining Rural Women", Social Welfare, March.
4. Kokila K (2001) "Credit GRO for Social Defense", Social Welfare May, 48;2,23.
5. Kopodia Karin (1997) "Mediating the Meaning of Market opportunities gender lost and class in Rural South India", Economic and Political Weekly.
6. Lalith N and B.S. Nagarajan (2002), " Self Help Groups in Rural Development", New Delhi, Dominant Publisher and Distributors.
7. Mani Mekalai .N and G Rajeswari (2002), groups roots Entrepreneurship through Self Help Groups (SHG). SEDMI Journal, vol.20, p.2.
8. Narayana Swamy N.S. Manivel and B. Bhaskar (2003), "Net working SHG and Co-Operatives In Analysis of strengths and weaknesses", Journal of Rural Development, vol.22, p-3.
9. Nair, Tara S. (1998), "Meeting the credit needs of the Micro Enterprise sector Issues in Focus", The Indian Journal of Labour Economics, July, September.

6

Micro Finance Programmes and Socio-Economic Development of Women – Case Study Analysis

Background

This chapter deals with the role of micro finance programmes in socio-economic development of women in Mandya district. A detailed case study analysis has been presented in this chapter. The analysis starts with the profile of Mandya district. Mandya district popularly known as 'Land of Sugar' came in to existence on 1st of July 1939. Earlier it was part of Mysore district. It is one of the districts with fertile land in south Karnataka..

The district is located in the south east of Karnataka State and shares its borders with the districts of Mysore, Hassan, Tumkur and Bangalore. Most of the land is flat, interspersed with hilly region and sparsely vegetated by thorns and bushes. The district is situated at the height of 762 to 914 meters from the sea level.

The district consists of 7 revenue blocks and for the easy educational administration the district is divided into 8 educational blocks. Total area of the district is 4961 square kms, out of which 3.11 lakh hectares are cultivated land, 0.24 lakh hectares are covered by forest area and remaining 1.63 lakh hectares are barren and uncultivable.

The prominent rivers that have influenced the life of the people of Mandya district are Cauvery, Hemavathi, Lokapavani, Simsha and Veera Vaishnavi. Branches of river Cauvery descends from the height of 200 feet at Shivanasamudra of Malavally taluk to form beautiful falls by name "Gaganachukki' and Bharachukki'. The famous Krishna Raja Sagara dam is built across the river Cauvery in Srirangapatna taluk and world famous "Brindavan Garden' is situated near the dam.

Soil of the district can be classified into three groups, such as,

- Red sandy loams
- Red clavey loams
- Clavey loams

These type of soils are suitable to cultivate different crops like sugarcane, Paddy, Ragi Jowar, ground nuts etc.

Socio Economic and Cultural Characteristics

Language: 'Kannada' is the prominent language of the district. But Urdu, Tamil, Telugu, Hindi, Marathi speaking people are there is the district.

Literature: The district has given so many great personalities to the filed of literature. Among them M.L. Srikantesha gowda, R. Narasimhachar, M.A. Ramanyengar, Alasingachar, B.M. Srikantaiah, M.R. Srinivasa murthy, Sitharama sasthry, A.N. Murthy rao, Pu. Thi.Na., H.L. Nage Gowda, Smt. Vani, Thriveni and Aryamba Pattabhi, Sithasutha, Dr. Besagara hally Ramanna and famous K.S. Narasimha swamy, Sobane Chikkamman, jee. Sham. Paramashivaiah are some of the prominent writers and authors of the district who were made the literary field rich.

Occupation : Agriculture is the major occupation in the district. The prominent crops are Sugarcane, Paddy, Ragi, Jowar, Groundnut, Sericulture and Coconut to som extent in K.R. Pet and Nagamangala taluk. Most of the people are depending on agriculture to earn their livelihood. Women folk also engaged themselves in Agriculture activity. Sugarcane and Paddy are the commercial crops and in recent days sericulture place a vital role in improving the economy of the district.

Industries: Since the sugarcane is the major crop in the district, there are four sugar factories, several khandasari sugar units and many Jaggery producing units. Milk products producing factory, edible oil producing factory, BPL battery factory and several small scale industries are there in the district.

Important Place: K.R. S. dam, Brindavan gardens, Sriranganatha temple, Rangana thittu and Kokkarre Belluru bird sanctuaries, Gaganachukki and Bharachukki water falls, Hemagiri, Muthethi, Shivanasamudra Hydro electric station (First in Asia), Tippu palace, Tippu fort, Melukote, Adi Chunchanagiri, Shivapura Sathyagraha Soudha are some of the prominent places which attracts tourist from different parts of the country.

Cultural Characteristics: Several local festivals gain important place in the district. Folk songs like Sobane, Jogula, Hacche, Suggi, Lavani etc., Folk dances like Nandi dhwaja, Path kunitha, Pooja Kunitha, Somana Kunitha, Mari Kunitha, Veera makkala kunitha, Panjina kunitha, Karagada kunitha, Onake kunitha, Garudi mela, Huli vesha, Kamsale etc., play a major role in the cultural history of the district.

Administrative Structure

District Level: Deputy Commissioner and the Chief Executive Officer are the district heads of Revenue and Zilla Panchayath respectively. More than 20 departments are working within perview of the Zilla Panchayath. Among them Education and Health are the important ones.

At district level Deputy Director of Public Instruction (Administration) and Deputy Director of Public Instruction (Development) are the Heads of the education department at district level.

Block Level: At taluka level Thahasildhar and the Taluk Panchayath Executive Officer are the Heads of the block. Block Education Officer looking after all responsibility related to educational administration and Block - Co-coordinator of BRCs taking care of In-service teacher training at the block level.

Village Level: Grama Panchayaths plays a vital role at the village level for all the developmental activities of the village. At village level in all the school there are School development and monitoring committees (SDMC) are established. It is the sub committee of Grama Panchayath which is taking care of the developmental activities.

Table - 6.1

Other General Information of the District are as follows:

Sl. No.	*Description*	*Numbers*
1.	Geographical area	4961 skm
2.	No. of Revenue Blocks	07
3.	No. Education Blocks	08
4.	No. of Habitations	2033
5.	No. of Grama Panchayaths	232
6.	No. of Town Panchayaths	05
7	No. of TMCs	04
8.	No. of CMCs	01
9.	No. of assembly constituencies	09
10.	No. of Loka Sabha constituency	01
11.	No. of Sub divisions	02

Source: District Gazetteer, Mandya.

Historical Profile

Srirangapatna, the island fortress of the legendary warrier Tiippu Sultan popularly known as "Tiger of Mysor" is just 25 K.M.s from Mandya city. Inside the fortress is Tippu's Mosque with its twin minarats, the celebrated Ranganatha Swamy temple, Tippu's summer palace, the Wellesley bridge and dungons where British officers were once imprisoned. Equally impressive is the ornate white domed Gumbaz, an imposing structure with dooms of ebony inlaid with ivory and lacquered with Tippu's Tiger - striped emblem. About 1 km. to the east of the fort, Tippu's summer palace known as the Dariadaulat bagh (Museum) is set amidst a lovely garden.

Demographic Profile

Population: As per 1991 census, the population of the district was 16.45lakhs. But as per 2001 census the population is increased to 17.53 lakhs with a decadal growth rate of 7.14, where s the decadal growth rate during 1981 to 1991 was 15.96, this clearly indicates that there is decrease in the growth rate of population in the district, which inturn reflects on child population. Decrease in growth rate is a very good indicator of successful implementation of family planning campaign.

Table - 6.2

Block wise/ gender wise population details

Sl. No.	*Name of the Revenue Block*	*Total Population*		
		Male	*Female*	*Total*
1.	K.R. Pet	123531	124714	248245
2.	Maddur	146707	144076	290783
3.	Malavally	143422	138387	281809
4.	Mandya	205798	199814	405612
5.	Nagamangala	94186	96584	190770
6.	Pandavapura	87458	87551	175009
7.	S.R. Patna	82625	110359	192984
	Total	883727	901485	1785212

Source: 2001 Census.

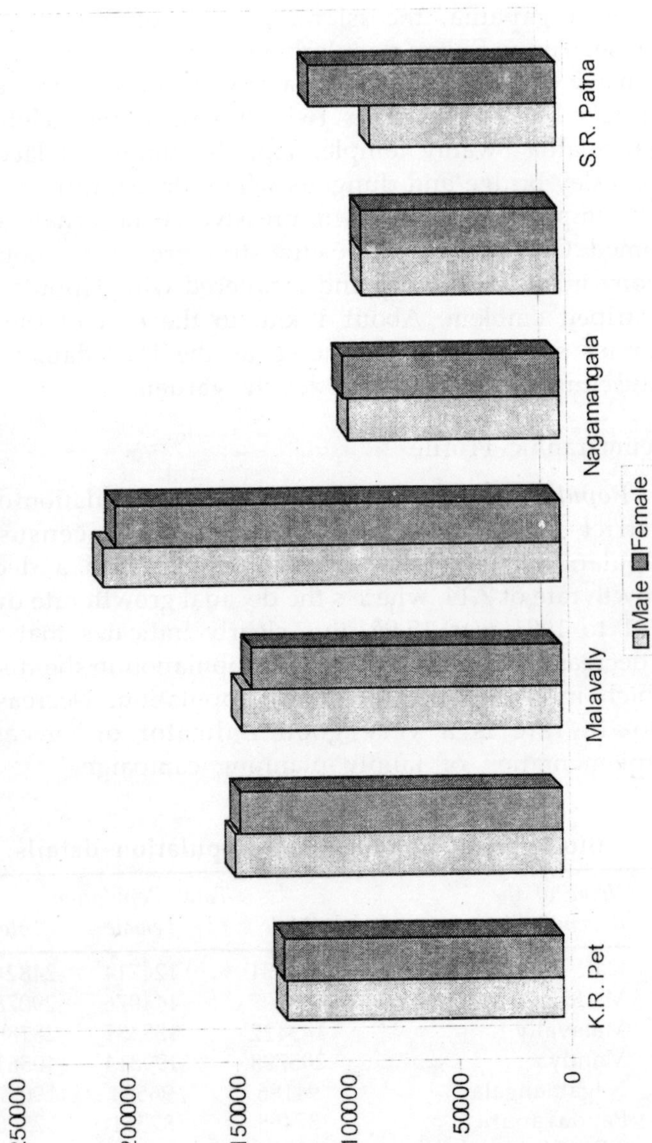
250000
200000
150000
100000
50000
0
K.R. Pet
Malavally
Nagamangala
S.R. Patna
Male
Female

Table - 6.3
Block wise Literacy details

Sl. No.	Name of the revenue Block	Literacy rate								
		1991 census			2001 census			Difference		
		M	F	T	M	F	T	M	F	T
1.	K.R. Pet	61.8	38.76	50.28	73.43	50.82	62.04	11.63	12.06	11.76
2.	Maddur	56.76	37.58	47.17	68.7	50.52	59.67	11.94	12.94	12.5
3.	Malavally	53.53	35.76	44.67	64.62	47.15	56.02	11.09	11.39	11.35
4.	Mandya	57.37	38.6	47.98	74.4	57.43	66.02	17.03	18.83	18.04
5.	Nagamangala	63.94	39.95	51.94	73.9	49.36	61.45	9.96	9.41	9.51
6.	Pandavapura	56.08	34.19	45.13	67.01	46.88	56.92	10.93	12.69	11.79
7.	S.R. Patna	57.84	41.9	49.87	71.13	54.98	63.13	13.29	13.08	13.26
	Total	58.19	38.11	48.15	70.46	51.02	60.75	12.27	12.91	12.60

Source: 2001 Census.

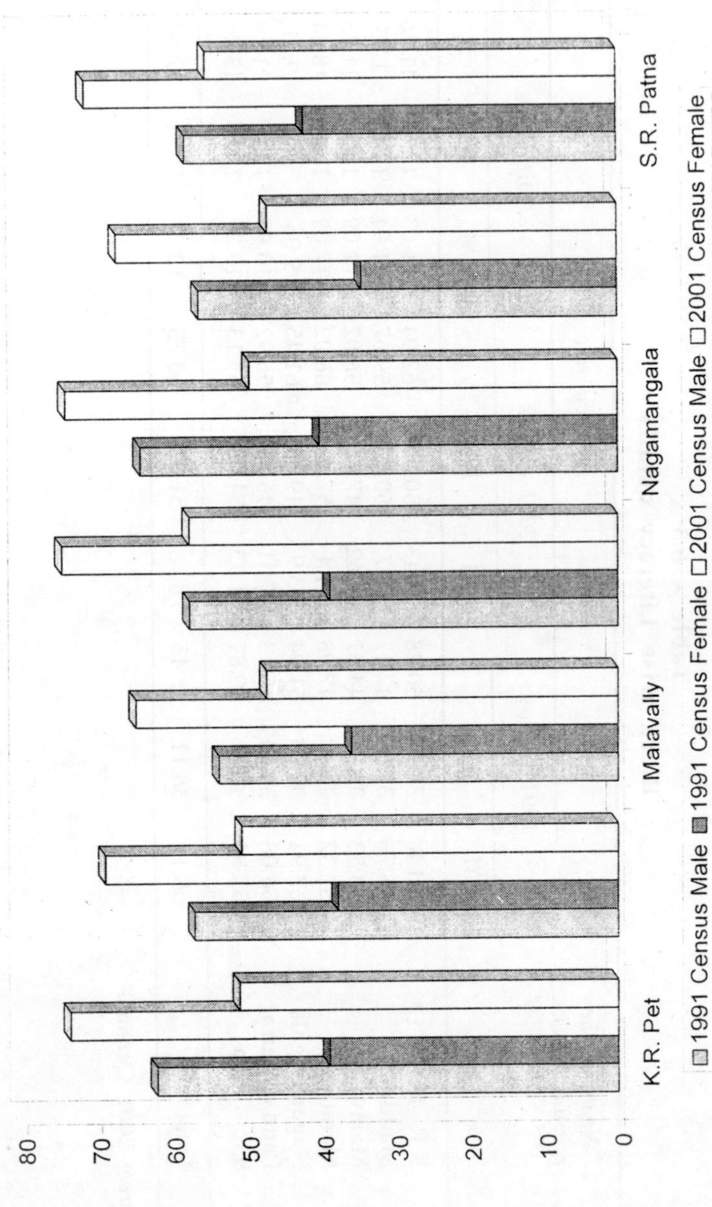
80
70
60
50
40
30
20
10
0
K.R. Pet
Malavally
Nagamangala
S.R. Patna
1991 Census Male
1991 Census Female
2001 Census Male
2001 Census Female

Literacy Scenario

Successful completion of Total literacy Campaign and proper implementation of DPEP, there is an increase in literacy rate by 12.06 in the last decade. In addition to these, good schooling facilities, attractive incentive schemes adapted in primary education and awareness among community are some of the factors contributing in increasing literacy rate. There is an almost equal increase in the literacy rate of Male and Female in the last decade, i.e., 12.27 and 12.91 respectively. Higher of 18.04% of literacy rate is increased in Mandya block and lowest of 9.51% in Nagamangala block during the last decade. At present there is an highest of 66.02% of literacy rate in Mandya taluk and lowest of 56.02% in Malavally taluk.

The district has seven taluks, 31 hoblies, 1,365 inhabited and 13 uninhabited villages and seven towns (as on 2002). The district has two revenue divisions with Mandya, Maddur and Malavalli taluks under Mandya Sub - division and Krishnarajpet, Nagamangala, Pandavapura and Srirangapatna taluks under Pandavapura sub - division. The geographical and the general information of Mandya district is given in table 6.4 and 6.5 and details of population census of 1991 is given in table 5.6 and provisional census statistics of 2001 is given in table - 6.7 and hobli - wise details of revenue villages are presented in table - 6.8.

Table - 6.4
Geographical details of Mandya District

Sl. No.	*Taluk*	*Area in Sq.km*	*East Longitude*		*North Latitude*	
			From	*To*	*From*	*To*
1.	K.R. Pet	905	76°19′	76°37′	12°28′	12°53′
2.	Maddur	618	76°42′	76°06′	12°24′	12°47′
3.	Malavalli	810	76°53′	76°07′	12°11′	12°29′

Sl. No.	Taluk	Area in Sq.km	East Longitude		North Latitude	
			From	To	From	To
4.	Mandya	716	76°42′	76°39′	12°21′	12°44′
5.	Nagamangala	1,045	76°34′	76°54′	12°38′	12°00′
6.	Pandavapura	540	76°28′	76°40′	12°21′	12°41′
7.	Srirangapatna	357	76°34′	76°53′	12°15′	12°29′
	District	4,991	76°19′	76°07′	12°11′	13°00′

Source: Mandya district at a Glance – 2000 -01

Table - 6.5
General particulars of Mandya district

Sl. No.	Taluk	Villages (As per 1991 Census)		Village Panchayats	City/ Urban agglomeration/ Municipality/ Corporation/ Notified areas	
					As per	
		Inhabited	Uninhabited	2000 -01	1991 Census	2000 -01
1.	K.R. Pet	296	20	34	1	1
2.	Maddur	153	7	42	1	1
3.	Malavalli	172	14	39	2	1
4.	Mandya	174	9	45	1	1
5.	Nagamangala	343	23	27	2	1
6.	Pandavapura	140	31	24	2	1
7.	Srirangapatna	87	9	21	2	1
	Total	1365	113	232	11	7

Source: Mandya District at A Glance – 2000-01, Zilla Panchayat 2000-01.

Table - 6.6
Taluk wise Area and Population of Mandya District
(As per 1991 Census)

Sl. No	*Taluk*		*Area Sq.km*	*Population*		
				Total	*Male*	*Female*
1	*2*	*3*	*4*	*5*	*6*	*7*
1.	K.R. Pet	Total	904.42	221,103	110,291	110,812
		Rural	900.16	203,104	100,870	102,234
		Urban	4.26	17,999	9,421	8,578
	K.R. Pet town Panchayat	Urban	4.26	17,999	9.421	8578
2.	Maddur Taluk	Total	618.43	282,726	144,572	138,154
		Rural	6120.73	260,611	133.243	127,368
		Urban	5.70	22,115	11,329	10.786
	Maddur Town l Municipal Counci	Urban	5.70	22,115	11,329	10.786
3.	Malavalli Taluk	Total	810.11	264,075	136,511	127,564
		Rural	807.54	226,971	117,519	109,452
	Belakavadi Mandal Panchayat	Urban	0.57	7,282	3,656	3,626
	Malavalli Town Municipal council	Urban	2.00	29,822	15,336	14,486
4.	Mandya Taluk	Total	715.90	383,030	196,759	185,271
		Rural	699.06	262,756	135,215	127,550
		Urban	16,84	120,265	62,544	57,721
	Mandya City Corporation	Urban	16,84	120,265	62,544	57,721
5.	Nagamangala	Total	1044.70	178,663	88,139	90,524
		Rural	1039.49	158,380	77,569	80,811
		Urban	5.21	20,283	10,570	9,713
	Bellur Mandal Panchayat	Urban	2.69	6,187	3,239	2,948
	Nagamangala Town Panchayat	Urban	2.52	14,096	7,331	6,765
6.	Pandavapur	Total	539.43	160,155	80,993	79,162
		Rural	530.81	140,903	71,152	69,751
		Urban	8.62	19,252	9,841	9,411

1	2	3	4	5	6	7
	Melukote Mandal Panchayat	Urban	4.28	3,254	1,655	1,599
	Pandavapura Town panchayat	Urban	4.34	15,998	8,186	7,812
7.	Srirangapatna	Total	353.81	146,741	75,270	71,471
		Rural	342.19	124,836	64,151	60,685
		Urban	11.62	21,905	11,119	10.786
	Srirangapatna Town Council	Urban	11.62	21,905	11,199	10.786
8.	Mandya District	Total	4961.00	1644,374	837,597	806,777
		Rural	4901.80	1388,570	699,719	677,851
		Urban	54.84	266,804	137,878	128,926
	Krishnarajasagar Notified Area	Urban	4.36	7,881	4,062	3,819

- Since the area of the three villages of Pandavapura and Srirangapatna taluks are included under the Krishnarajasagara Notified Area, it has been shown separately

Source: Census of India 1991, Part 12-B, Mandya District Census, Series – 11, Karnataka.

Table - 6.7
Details of Provisional population as per 2001 Census

Sl. No	*Taluk*		*Area Sq.km*	*Population*		
				Total	*Male*	*Female*
1	2	3	4	5	6	7
1.	K.R. Pet	Total	904.42	247,757	123,271	124,468
		Rural	900.16	225,284	111,705	113,579
		Urban	4.26	22,473	11,566	10,907
	K.R. Pet town Panchayat	Urban	4.26	22,473	11,566	10,907
2.	Maddur Taluk	Total	618.43	289,704	146,110	143,594
		Rural	612.73	263,248	132,723	130,525
		Urban	5.70	26,456	13,387	13,069

1	2	3	4	5	6	7
	Maddur Town Municipal Council	Urban	5.70	26,456	13,387	13,069
3.	Malavalli Taluk	Total	810.11	281,345	143,124	138,221
		Rural	807.54	245,545	124,837	120,708
		Urban	2.57	35,800	18,287	17,513
	Malavalli Town Municipal council	Urban	2.57	35,800	18,287	17,513
4.	Mandya Taluk	Total	715.90	405,898	206,199	199,199
		Rural	699.06	274,687	139,569	135,118
		Urban	16,84	131,211	66,630	64,581
	Mandya City Corporation	Urban	16,84	131,211	66,630	64,581
5.	Nagamangala	Total	1044.70	190,814	94,282	96,532
		Rural	1039.49	174,764	86,076	87,688
		Urban	5.21	16,050	8,206	7,844
	Nagamangala Town Panchayat	Urban	5.21	16,050	8,206	7,844
6.	Pandavapura	Total	539.43	175,008	82,520	87,488
		Rural	530.81	156,772	78,309	78,463
		Urban	8.62	18,236	9,211	9,025
	Pandavapura Town panchayat	Urban	8.62	18,236	9,211	9,025
7.	Srirangapatna	Total	353.81	162,682	82,472	80,210
		Rural	342.19	139,234	70,528	68,706
		Urban	11.62	23,448	11,944	11,504
	Srirangapatna Town Council	Urban	11.62	23,448	11,944	11,504
8.	Mandya District	Total	4961.00	17,61,718	887,307	874,411
		Rural	4897.44	14,79,534	734,747	735,787
		Urban	59.20	282,184	143,560	138,624
	Krishna-rajasagar Notified Area	Urban	4.36	8,510	4,329	4,181

Note:1. The Talukwise area figures are for the reporting area for land utilization purposes as worked out by State Survey Department. The Geographical area of the district is computed. by the Survey of India. So the total figures of the taluk do not tally with the total figures for areas.

2. Krishnarajasagar Notified area has been converted into Grama Panchayat in March, 2002 by the Government. Still as per the census of 2001, Krishnarajasagar has been considered as Notified area. Of the present seven urban areas of the district, there is one Corporation (Mandya), three Municipalities (Maddur, Malavalli and Srirangapatna) and three Town Panchayats K.R. Pet, Pandavapura and Nagamangala).

Table - 6.8
The details of Hobli - wise Revenue villages, of the district (Inclusive of up-inhabited villages) - 2001

Taluk	*Hobli*	*Villages*
	Mandya Sub-Division	
1. Mandya	1. Mandya	17
	2. Kottatti	35
	3. Dudda	54
	4. Basaralu	50
	5. Keragodu	27
	Total	**183**
2. Maddur	1. Maddur	43
	2. Chikkarasinakere	43
	3. Koppa	44
	4. Atakooru	33
	Total	**162**
3. Malavalli	1. Malavalli	51
	2. Halaguru	45
	3. Boppagowdanapura	45
	4. Kirugavalu	45
	Total	**186**
4. Pandavapura	1. Pandavapura	57
	2. Chinakuruli	65
	3. Melukote	49
	Total	171
5. K.R. Pet	1. K.R. Pet	51
	2. Santhebachahalli	59

Taluk	*Hobli* *Mandya Sub-Division*	*Villages*
	3. Shilanere	52
	4. Bhookanakere	48
	5. Akkihebbal	49
	6. Kikkeri	57
	Total	**316**
6. Nagamangala	1. Nagamangala	64
	2. Devalapura	63
	3. Honakere	82
	4. Bindiganavile	75
	5. Bellur	82
	Total	**366**
7. Srirangapatna	1. Srirangapatna	17
	2. Belagola	20
	3. Kurubara Shettyhalli	27
	4. Arakere	31
	Total	**95**

Source: District Gazetteer, Mandya.

In Mandya district there are 4780 Stree Shakti Self-Help Groups are formed with 67,764 women members. Total savings accumulated Rs.1,22, 37,000 and Rs. 4, 90, 24,000 loan amount was taken by these groups and government has been granted Rs.6, 24,000 as a revolving fund.

The agriculture in the district is developed. With assured canal irrigation facilities, the land productivity is high and double cropping is assured in the whole of district, in general, and in particular. Hence, banks consider investment on crop production to be safe. However, the formal banks did not provide credit to improve occupational diversification among agricultural households both on account of profitability considerations and the perception that those who were unemployed and underemployed from the agricultural labourer households were lazy .

Case Study Analysis

Here we have made an attempt to analyse the role of NGOs like Vikasama, MRD (MYRADA) and CDS(Community Development Society) in Mandya district of Karnataka State in catering the needs of the women. These three non-governmental institutions actively participated in improving the livelihood security of women through self help groups in Mandya district. Table - 6.9 shows the reasons given by the members for Joining the SHGs about 37 percent of them opined that they joined the group of promoting savings and for getting loans. Thirty-one percent of them gave multiple reasons like getting loan, inculcating the savings habit, and welfare of the family. In CDS about one-third reported that they were attracted to the group by the possibility of easy access to the formal credit system and opportunity to raise loans.

Table - 6.9
Motivating factors-Members perception

Reasons	*MRD*	*CDS*	*Vikasama*	*All class*
For getting loan	2(6)	17(33)	7(7)	26(14)
For promoting Savings habit	2(6)	9(16)	5(9)	16(9)
For availing loan andPromoting savings habit	9(26)	11(21)	49(50)	69(37)
For family's welfare	-	2(4)	-	2(1)
Other reasons	4(11)	4(7)	4(7)	13(8)
Multiple reasons	18(52)	10(19)	31(31)	59(31)
Total	**35(100)**	**53(100)**	**98(100)**	**186(100)**

Source: Field Survey. (figures in brackets are percentages)

Only two members reported that they joined the group for the welfare of their families about eight percent thought that membership in the group would raise their status in society as one of the reason for joining the group.

Group size

A group self not more than 30 members to suggested as ideal for forging solidity among members and for effective monitoring of their performance. The CDS groups had membership in the range of 10 to 49 in MRD groups, membership is strictly restricted to a maximum of 20 persons, when membership exceeds 20 persons new groups are formed at the imitative of MRD by co-opting more new members. New members desirous of joining MRD are admitted to groups which have only less than 20 members. The group size of Vikasama ranges from 13 to 39 members.

Unlike other voluntary agencies, in Vikasama two or more persons from the same may join the group. This may not be desirably as financially better off families could thereby dominate and manipulate the groups decisions. The unit constituted at a locality want level has around 10 to 15 SHGs. The unit exercise external control over the SHGs coming under its purview.

Group meetings and attendance

The practice of holding regular group meetings is found to build better understanding forge solidarity and develop qualities of self-help and mutual help among the members to Vikasama the group meetings are held only once in a month. The group leaders spied that the practice was decided upon unanimously an all the members were occupied in various activities. It is also seen that the percentage of attendance varied from 60 to 70 percent. The monthly meeting. This usually lasts for about an hour, discusses common issues including local problems, like treatment of the member disease of coconut and problems of law voltage of the electricity distribution.

In MRD, almost all the groups bold weekly meetings on a fixed day and time. The survey revealed that about

70-90 percent of the members attended the meetings regularly. The functionaries insist on holding regular weekly meetings.

In CDS we found differences in performance across groups in well performing groups attendance in meetings was around 40 to 60 percent, while in unsuccessful groups it was below 30 percent. In unsuccessful groups, meetings were not held regularly. Some members sent their savings to the group through children or other members. Many of the members opined that other than thrift and credit transactions no serious agenda was discussed at meetings. Meetings were therefore found monotonous and members tended to keep away from meetings. Other factors like loss of faith in the group leader had also led to poor attendance in a few cases. The leaders play a prominent role in motivating members to attend regularly. It is observed that the tempo of meetings could be maintained if other issues including local and personal (familiar) issues are also discussed along issues relating to thrift and credit. The enthusiasm seen among the members of the older groups in the beginning could not be retained at alter stages due to the failure of groups to rise to their expectations.

The idea of imposing fine (with the groups' consent) for unauthorized absence may be thought of for maintaining the attendance rate. Moreover, reading the minutes of the previous meeting in the group by members on a rotation basis might help in improving the articulation skill of members and would motivate the less educated members to improve their learning and take over leadership role of the group.

Record maintenance

The CDS byelaw states that four records are to be statutorily maintained. In all the CDS groups visited, we could see that this function is done systematically. The introduction of Management Information system (MIS) since January 2000 has improved the monitoring system.

The Panchayat Coordinator is expected to submit a monthly report of all NHGs before the fifth of every subsequent month to the President of the Panchayat CDS who in turn will present it to the district CDS, for monitoring and evaluation.

However, the system of accounts maintenance and book-keeping is found to be the best and the most systematic in MRD groups, may be because of the presence of more bank-linked groups and their close liaison with Vishveswaraya Grameen Bank. The stipulation that the monthly report/statement is to be presented to the MRD office on the 2nd of every month makes the maintenance of records effective. In Shreyas also there is regular monitoring and evaluation. However, in Vikasama, in some of the groups men maintained the accounts on half the women's group, thus hampering the women empowerment process.

Thrift

We have seen that thrift is a very important indicator of a group's success because consistent growth in thrift is a clear indication of the growing confidence of the members in the group. Collection of shrift is a major activity of the SHGs, carried out successfully since their inception in all the three groups. The poor who need many for purchase of various consumption goods quite often meet their contingencies by borrowing from professional money-lenders and others at high rates of interest. SHGs have been extremely effective in creating the habit of savings among the rural poor and mobilizing it for common good.

A fixed amount (not in CDS) as decided by the members is collected as thrift during the group meeting. The member's savings are entered in their passbooks as well as in the savings account maintained in the group. The amounts of monthly savings varied with the socio-economic status of members. Earlier several members who were not having any income of their own had depended on their husbands for remitting the thrift amount, A few of them had even discontinued their membership in course of time when their husbands failed to give them money for remittance in the thrift account.

In some CDS groups, members were seen remitting the credit repayment statements only after availing Joan from the group. There are instances where members had left the groups because they felt that the thrift collected in the weekly meeting were not deposited by the leaders in the bank, but were rolling it for other purpose. When a member loses confidence, naturally the remittance in the thrift account.

In some CDS groups, members were seen remitting the credit repayment installment only after availing loan from the group. There are instances where members had left the groups because they felt that the thrift collected in the weekly meeting were not deposited by the leaders in the bank. But were rolling it for other purposes. When a member loses confidence, naturally the rumor spreads like fire and eventually leads to group failure.

In successful groups some of the members were found unhappy as they felt that their thrift was not earning any interest while they had to pay interest for thrift loans. However, despite of the problems, a redeeming feature observed is that SHGs were able to mobilize rural saving quite satisfactorily from the members. They seemed to have developed the habit of saving among the poor, a fact which had been earlier thought of as impossible.

Credit

The success and effectiveness of intermediaries like SHGs is determined largely by the extent to which they have been able to create for their members a reliable and easy source of borrowing for households and productive purposes. The SHG strategy has helped these members who are from the weaker sections to gain easy access to institutional credit. For the formal credit agency, lending with minimal transaction cost and reaching a large member of poor with assured repayment, sounds great in the present context of the declining credit deposit ratio in the state. Besides the monetary element, the lending operation enable the groups to learn the way of prioritizing and identifying their felt needs, enforcing credit terms and conditions and monitoring loan utilization and repayment.

It is generally conceived that thrift amount can be used for consumption soothing meeting small consumption requirements, such as expenses towards marriage, funeral, medical treatment, and repayment of debt, whereas loans taken from external agencies are meant mainly for pursuing income-generating activities. However, this norm is not strictly followed as in some successful groups the members were found using the thrift amount only for economic activities and doing without external borrowings. These groups feel that the money they raised should not be lost in the form of interest payment on external borrowings.

In some other groups bank loans taken for productive purpose were used for conducting marriages, with the knowledge of their group leaders and members, (decided and approved in the weekly meeting) as the loanees were in urgent need of money for meeting the marriage. Related expenses. When asked why she did not take loan from thrift, a member who had thus utilized bank loan for marriage reported that able only Rs.1,200 in her thrift balance while the bank loan sanctioned to the group was Rs.5000, such instances which defeat the entire purpose of self-help were found common in many groups. There is thus need for sensitizing the members on the effective end use of credit. The group leaders have to ensure that the production loan taken is not squandered on unproductive uses.

In Vikasama, the rate of interest was comparatively

low (12 percent) and the average credit amount sanctioned was high, facility which motivated large members to join the Vikasama groups. In MRD and CDS groups, the rate of interest varied from 18 to 24 percent as stipulated by NABARD Several members appear to have found even 24 percent interest per annum relatively cheap on comparison with the rates charged by moneylenders. The groups retained a margin ranging from 6 to 12 percent. This margin acts as a cushion against default risk, if any, because even if a member defaults, the groups/voluntary agencies have to repay the amount to the lending institution.

In CDS besides 12 bank-linked groups several groups had obtained loans from RMK and Panchayat Fund. In SBM besides bank loan, members had availed credit from IC and Panchayat Fund in Vikasama none of the groups were linked to banks Vikasama functionaries said that they had not approached banks since they were having sufficient funds from various other agencies. They are mainly using the funds from credit Union, HUDCO, and IC, besides local resources.

In Shreyas, some of the members were having recurring deposit and fixed deposit, an indicator of the fact that all the numbers did not holding to the category of 'poor' Members very generally of the view that the credit went to the members of particular community though the co-ordinates said that was not the case. Among the three voluntary agencies, the CDS is found to have been the most effective in pooling resources and initiating action due probably to she fact that it is sponsored by the government.

Leadership

The presence of a strong, dynamic leader has been identified as the most significant factor for the successful functioning and sustainability of SHG. Usually a person with some previous experience of competence to discharge the various financial responsibilities of SHG is selected as the leader. The leadership training imparted to the selected mₑmbers enabled them to discharge their duties with case, we were really amazed at the enthusiasm of several leaders despite the fact that the post is not remunerative though some find a burden, a large proportion of the present leaders seem to have taken their role as an opportunity for self-less service to the society.

In Vikasama, it was observed that many elders had been holding positions in CDS or other SHGs. In CDS groups though there is a five member elected term to manage the groups, except the President and the Secretary, the where are there only in name, without taking part in any activity of the group. Though the CDS byelaw states that the leaders are to be elected afresh once in two years, in 82 percent of the groups studied, the same leaders are found to have been in office since their inception. The CDS president remarked that " this is due to the absence of educated persons or persons with ability to run the group.

In MRD their previous experience in Mahila Samaja helped the leaders to managing the present group effectively. The presence of young graduates in MRD had a positive impact on its growth. The leaders are elected re-elected annually.

The president and the co-ordinations of the *Panchayat* CDS helped many groups in getting the maximum financial benefit, benefit, in solving conflicts and in initiating social activities. Anyhow, a few groups complained about the bias of the ADS chairperson in favour of their own groups in distributing credit and other facilities. We observe that in the NHGs of the CDS president and the chairpersons, around 50 percent of the members were having economic activities, while the percentage of members with income generating programmes in other NHGs was comparatively low.

Table - 6.10

Members perception on assuming leadership role

Perception	*Number*	
Interested	54	(45)
Not interested	102	(55)
Total	**186**	**(100)**

Source: Field survey, Figures in brackets are percentages to total

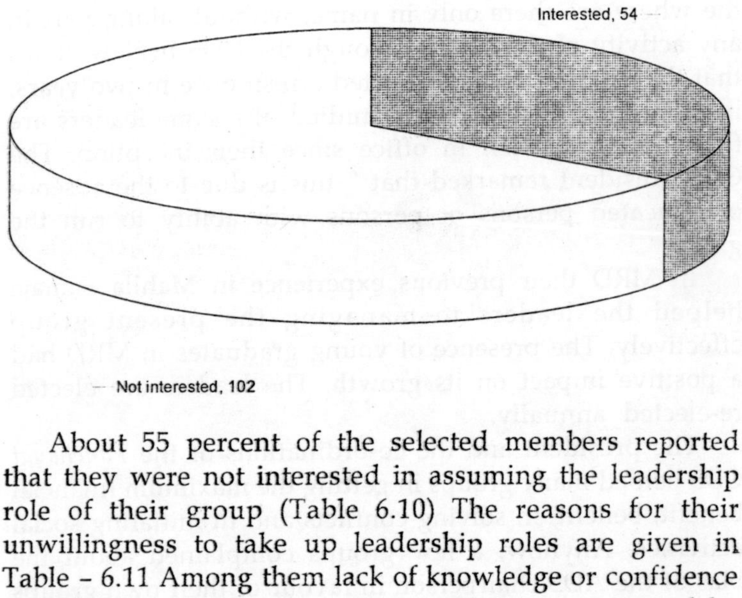

About 55 percent of the selected members reported that they were not interested in assuming the leadership role of their group (Table 6.10) The reasons for their unwillingness to take up leadership roles are given in Table - 6.11 Among them lack of knowledge or confidence was the most important reason since it was reported by 68 percent.

Among the members of Vikasama 43 percent reported that they had no time on were not interested in taking leadership responsibilities. In CDS, members (44 percent) remarked that they were not educated enough to write the minutes and accounts and manage the group. A few Muslim members felt that mobility outside their locality may be a problem if they accept the leadership position. In MRD, members preformed to have the same leaders re-elected In case of continued leadership it was found that members reposed confidence in the leadership and its guidance and did not want to change it. Their strong faith and trust in.

Table – 6.11
Reasons for abstaining from Leadership

Factors	*MRD*	*CDS*	*Vikasama*	*All class*
Lack of confidence	2(11)	7(17)	1(2)	10(10)
Lack of knowledge	2(11)	14(33)	15(36)	31(30)
Knowledge	8(44)	11(26)	8(19)	27(27
No time/Not willing toTake responsibility	-	10(24)	18(43)	28(27)
Multiple response	6(24)	-	-	6(6)
Total	**18(100)**	**42(100)**	**42(100)**	**102(100)**

Source: Field survey; Figures in brackets are percentages.

The leadership is reflected in their words, "It is because of her that we are able to perform smoothly". The fact remains, however, that unless all members took up leadership by turns, empowerment may be confined to only the group leaders and will not spread to all the members. In one of the MRD groups, it was found that the leader followed an "autocratic" to be effective in getting the maximum financial assistance to the group members and in ensuring prompt repayment of loans.

In the majority of cases it is found that only the leaders are clear and are aware of the goals and the concept of SHG, and the information and training which they receive from the high level meetings is not effectively passed on to the members. Leaders are trained on various topics, the benefits of which do not always peculate to them.

Socio-economic profile of the selected members

In this part the demographic, socio-economic and other characteristics of the selected members are presented.

Table -6.12 gives the group-wise age composition of the selected members. It is seen that 62 percent of the selected members were in the age group of 30-45 years, which is considered to be the most productive period in a person's life. The proportions of members in the age group of less than 30years and those than 45 years were 19 each.

Table - 6.12

Agency-wise Distribution of Members by Age Group

Age	*MRD*	*CDS*	*Vikasama*	*All class*
Loss than 30 years	6(17)	12(23)	17(17)	35(19)
35-45 years	22(63)	33(62)	61(63)	116(62)
Above 45 years	35(100)	53(100)	98(100)	186(100)
Total	**35(100)**	**53(100)**	**98(100)**	**186(100)**

Source: Field survey Figures it brackets as percentages.

As per the Census Report 2001, the average family size to the district is 6.49. During the field survey we have observed that majority of the Muslim families were having more than three children.

Table - 6.13

Agency-wise Distribution of Members by Family Size

Family size	*MRD*	*CDS*	*Vikasama*	*All class*
Less than 3	7(20)	19(19)	18 (19)	35(19)
3 to 5	23(66)	32(60)	60(61)	115(62)
Above 5	5(14)	11(21)	20(20)	36(19)
Total	**35(100)**	**53(100)**	**98(100)**	**186(100)**

Source: Field survey, Figures in brackets are percentages.

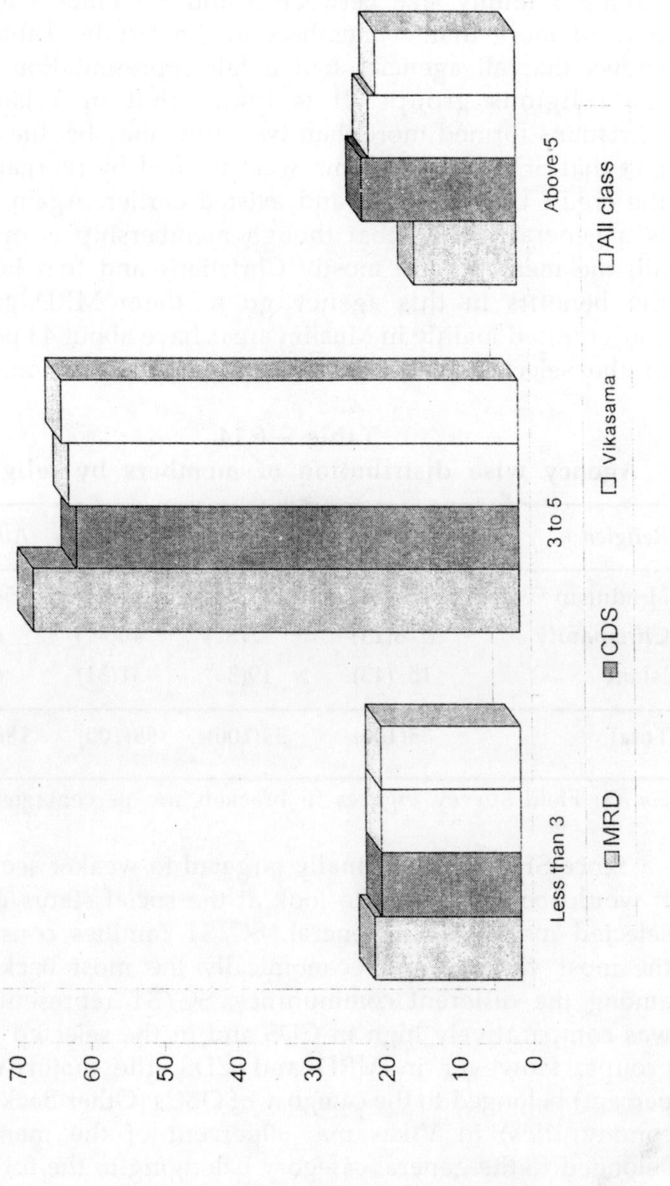
70
60
50
40
30
20
10
0
Less than 3
3 to 5
Above 5
MRD
CDS
Vikasama
All class

However, among the selected members 62 percent were having a family size between 3 and 5 members and 19 percent more than 5 members in the family. Table 6.14 shows that all agencies had a fair representation of all the religious groups. It is found that in Vikasama, Christians formed more than two-fifths may be due to the fact that SHGs of Vikasama were formed by reorganizing the credit Union, which and existed earlier. Again, there is a general feeling that though membership is open to all, the members are mostly Christians and that built of the benefits in this agency go to them MRD groups concentrated mainly in Muslim areas have about 43 percent of the selected members belonging to the community.

Table - 6.14
Agency wise distribution of members by religion

Religion	*MRD*	*CDS*	*Vikasama*	*All class*
Hinduism	12 (34)	17(32)	27(28)	56 (30)
Christianity	8(23)	17(32)	40(41)	65(35)
Islam	15 (43)	19(36)	31(31)	65(35)
Total	**35(100)**	**53(100)**	**98(100)**	**186(100)**

Source: Field survey Figures in brackets are percentages

Since SHG is conceptually targeted to weaker sections. It would be interesting to look at the social status of the selected members. In general, SC/ST families constitute the most variable and economically the most backward among the different communities, SC/ST representation was comparatively high in CDS and in the selected MRD groups. However in MRD and CDS, the majority (53 percent) belonged to the category of OBCs (Other Backward communities) in Vikasama, 60percent of the members belonged to the general category belonging to the forward status of the society.

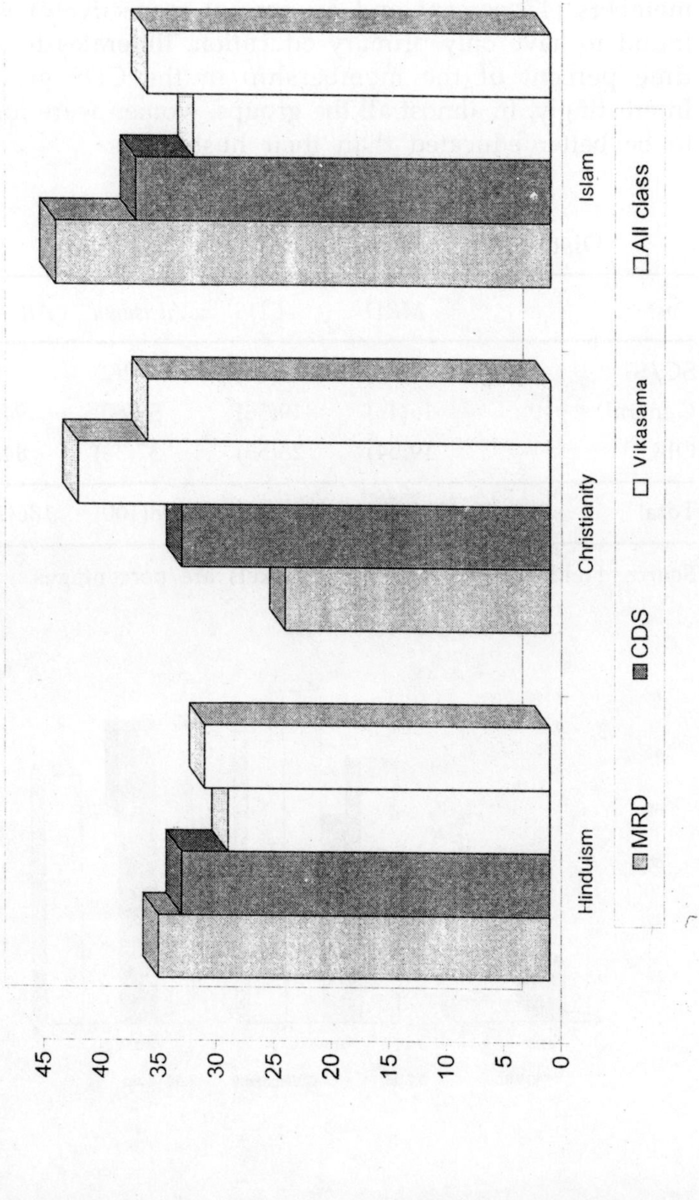
0
5
10
15
20
25
30
35
40
45
Hinduism
Christianity
Islam
MRD
CDS
Vikasama
All class

Table 6.15 shows that the members of Vikasama groups were more educated than the members of other groups. Forty-four percent of them had qualifications of SSLC or above. In CDS and MRD, the majority of the selected members (47 percent and 35 percent respectively) were found to have only primary education. Illiterates formed time percent of the membership in the CDS groups. Interestingly. In almost all the groups, women were found to be better educated than their husbands.

Table - 6.15
Distribution of members by social status

Caste	*MRD*	*CDS*	*Vikasama*	*All class*
SC/ST	-	6(11)	2(2)	8(4)
General	16(46)	19(36)	59(60)	94(51)
OBC	19(54)	28(53)	37(33)	84(45)
Total	35(100)	53(100)	98(100)	186(100)

Source: Field survey figures is brackets are percentages.

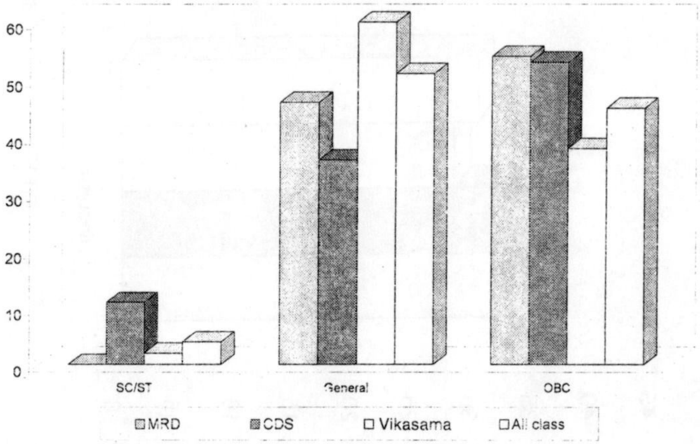

Table - 6.16
Distribution of Members by Level of Education

Education level	*MRD*	*CDS*	*Vikasama*	*All class*
Illiterate/ No response	1(3)	5(9)	5(5)	11(6)
Literate	3(9)	4(8)	10(10)	17(9)
Primary	13(37)	25(47)	28(29)	66(35)
High school	7(20)	8(15)	12(12)	27(15)
SSLC	6(17)	8(15)	33(34)	47(25)
Above SSLC	5(14)	7(6)	10(10)	18(10)
Total	15(100)	53(100)	98(100)	186(100)

Source: Field survey Figure is brackets are percentages.

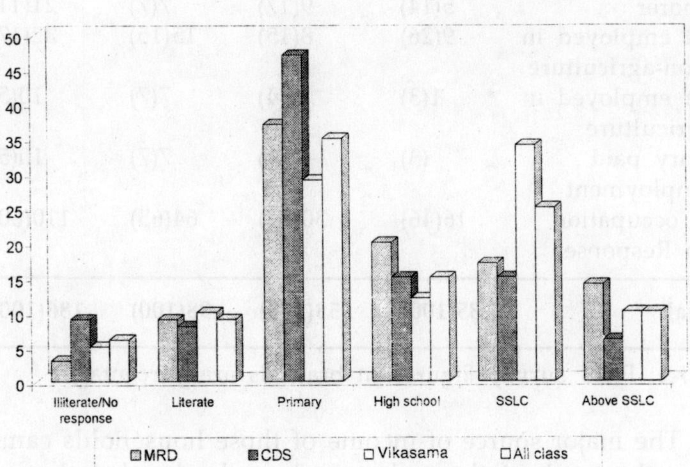

Most of the members were found to be either agricultural laborers or self-employed workers seventeen percent of the members had their own small-scale units, run on self-employment basis engaged in non-agricultural activates (Table - 6.17) In Vikasama 65 percent of the members remained unemployed, while the corresponding figure in MRD was only 46 percent. Two-fifties of the members in CDS groups had some occupation or other, through the returns from them were not up to their expectations. It may be noted that despite the fact that ample funds are available for economic activities. It may be noted that despite the fact that ample funds are available for economic activities 60 percent of the total sample was still not having any occupation

Table - 6.17
Group-wise Activity Status of Beneficiaries

Activity status	*MRD*	*CDS*	*Vikasama*	*All class*
Laborer	5(14)	9(17)	7(7)	21(11)
Self employed in Non-agriculture	9(26)	8(15)	15(15)	32(17)
Self employed in agriculture	1(3)	2(4)	7(7)	10(5)
Salary paid Employment	(3)	1(4)	7(7)	10(5)
No occupation no Response	16(46)	30(57)	64(65)	110(60)
Total	**35(100)**	**53(100)**	**98(100)**	**186(100)**

Source: Field survey Figures in brackets are percentages

The major source of income of those households came from the work of the male members, husband, father or others. Table 6.18 shown that 62 percent of the members feature of the members of the CDS groups is that for 16 percent among them, spouses had either deceased of were non-working.

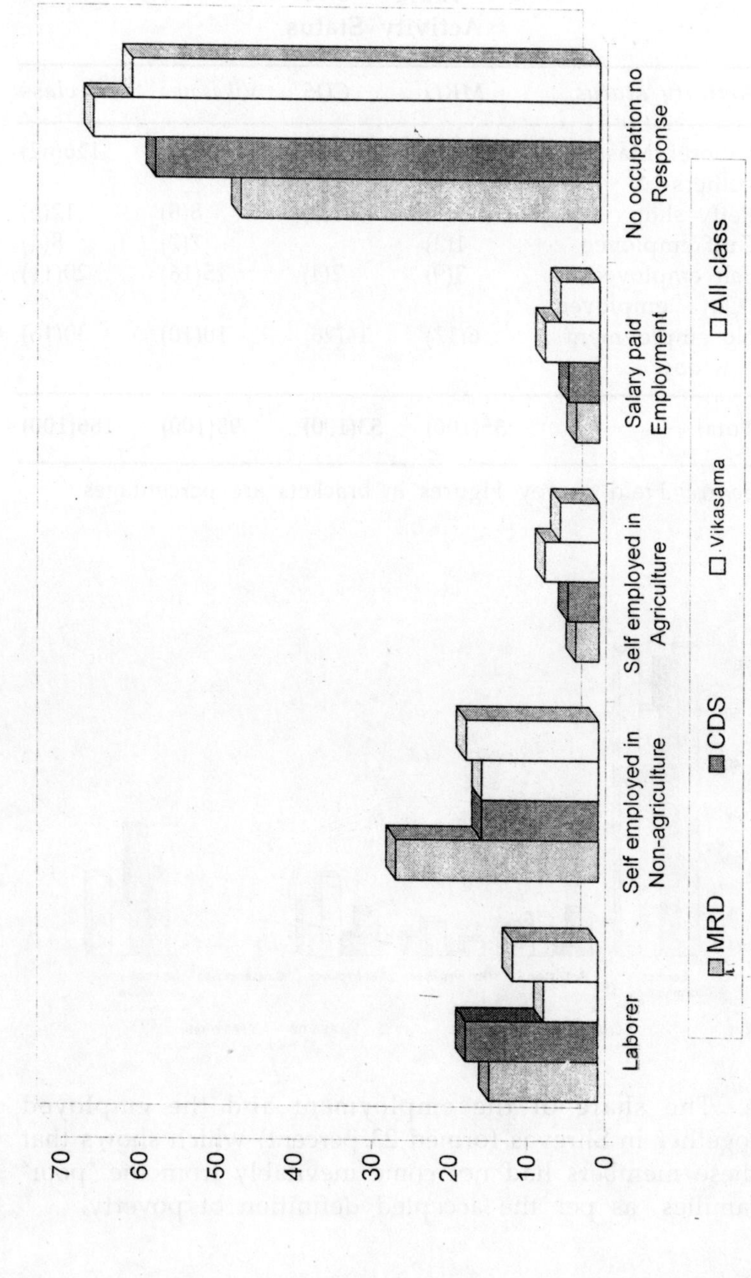
70
60
50
40
30
20
10
0
Laborer
Self employed in Non-agriculture
Self employed in Agriculture
Salary paid Employment
No occupation no Response
MRD
CDS
Vikasama
All class

Table - 6.18
Activity Status

Activity status	*MRD*	*CDS*	*Vikasama*	*All class*
Laborer Mason/ others	22(63)	16(600)	58(50)	116(62)
Petty shop	3(9)	1(2)	8(8)	12(6)
Gulf employee	1(3)	-	7(7)	8(4)
Self employee, Govt. employee	3(9)	2(4)	15(16)	20(11)
No employment widow	6(17)	14(26)	10(10)	30(16)
Total	**35(100)**	**53(100)**	**98(100)**	**186(100)**

Source: Field survey Figures in brackets are percentages.

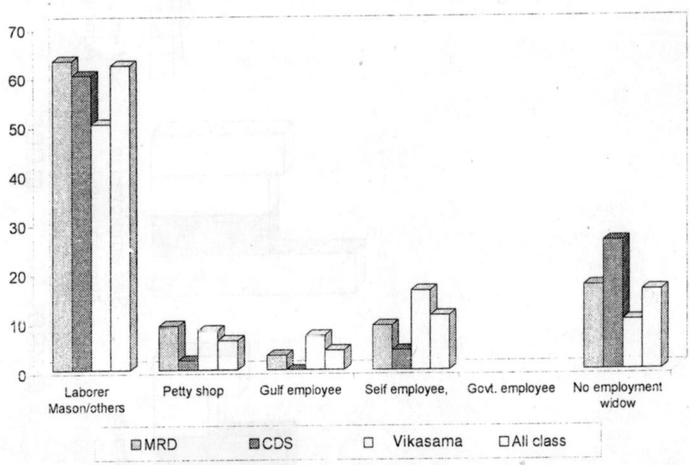

The share of the employment and the employed together in Shreyas formed 23 percent) which shows that these members had not come inevitably from the 'poor' families, as per the accepted definition of poverty.

Table - 6.19
Distribution of Members by Monthly Family Income

Monthly Income	*MRD*	*CDS*	*Vikasama*	*All class*
Less than Rs.2000	3(9)	14(26)	10(10)	27(15)
Rs.2000-4000	23(66)	20(38)	46(47)	89(49)
Rs.4000-6000	8(23)	18(34)	26(27)	52(28)
Above 6000	1(3)	1(2)	16(16)	18(10)
Total	**35(100)**	**53(100)**	**98(100)**	**186(100)**

Source: Field survey Figures in brackets are percentages.

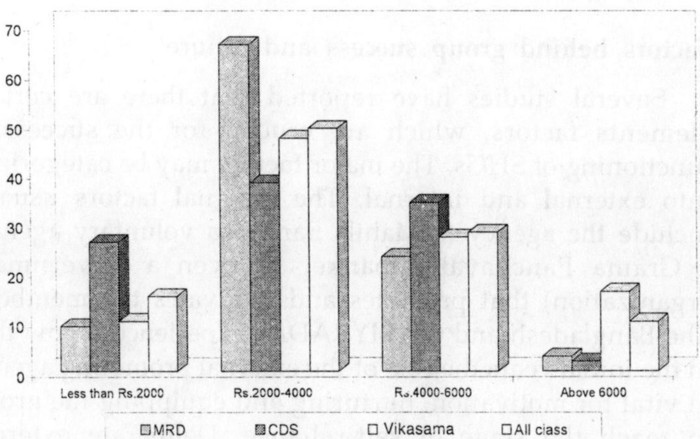

A family with monthly income of above Rs.1500 is treated as a family belonging in the above poverty line (APL) We could find that only a very few members come under this category. Table - 6.19 shows that in CDS. 26 percent of the selected sample members reported their monthly family income as below Rs.2000. In the other two, the corresponding proportions were much lower. Thus the CDS groups catered to the seeds of the poor to a larger extent then the other groups.

In Vikasama 43 percent of the members were having more than Rs.4000 as family income of them. 16 percent reported incomes more than Rs.6000. These higher income families had their numbers engaged in several occupation -compactors, auto-drivers, teachers, clerks at tenders in government offices newspaper agents and LIC gents. The sons of a few old members were reportedly working to Gulf countries or were well-employed in India. Only 15 percent of the total members in the sample reported their family income as less than Rs.2000. Thus it may be inferred that the SHGs have either improved of the economic conditions of a fairly good number of BPL families of that the members of SHGs were drawn also from families belonging to the APL category.

Factors behind group success and failure

Several studies have reported that there are certain elements factors, which are crucial for the successful functioning of SHGs. The major factors may be categorized into external and internal. The external factors usually include the agency (a Mahila Samaja a voluntary agency, a Grama Panchayat a banker or even a Government organization) that promotes and motivates the members. The Bangladesh and the MYRADAs experiences show that in the initial years the role of the external promoting agency in vital for motivation, nurturing and equipping the group to reach the stage of self-reliance. Deliberate external intervention of the promoting agency (in the initial stage) has helped in laying a strong foundation in the MYRADA group. However whether it is the government or the voluntary organization, the role of the promoting agency is not confined to mere mobilization of rural women folk. The agency is also expected to inculcate in them a spirit of self-help and mutual help and a profound understanding of the mission and goals of the SHG.

Groups cannot be built overnight. Group formation is a slow, time-consuming process. Once the members get the crux of the mission and realize the benefits, they would remain loyal throughout and never leave the group. When the group becomes stabilized in its functioning, internal factors like good leadership, unity and mutual understanding among the members determine the pace of growth and development. The internal factors contributing to group success include (i) presence of an educated, sincere, and dynamic leader (ii)stability in leadership (iii) homogeneity in membership (members belonging to same income or social strata) (iv) democracy and transparency and (v) co-operation, unity and mutual understanding Based on these coteries, We have identified a few internal and external factors which have influenced the functioning of the selected groups under the three agencies.

The details given in Table 6.20 give the members perceptions on factors behind group success. It comes out that the role of the promoting agency and the co-coordinator are the most important external factors contributing to the success of the group. Forty-six percent of the members interviewed felt that the promoting agency and the co-co-ordinators had crucial role in the initial years till the groups reach the stage of self-sufficiency. However a MRD, the role of the bank and the promoting agency was highlighted by 54 percent of the members. In CDS, 25 percent gave multiple responses and 23 percent did not respond or were neutral. While considering the internal factors contributing to group's success group wise variations were not observed-69 percent of the members, interceptive of groups, remarked that good leadership, co-operation among members and transparency in decision making are essential for the smooth functioning and sustainability of the group. However member felt that the role of the group leader is one among the foremost factors responsible for a group' success or failure. In some of the defunct groups, absence of a strong secretary to in calculate in the members the real spirit of group dynamics had led to its failure.

Table - 6.20

Members perception about factors contributing to groups success

Contributing factors external factors	*MRD*	*CDS*	*Vikasama*	*All class*
Promoting agency	5(14)	9(17)	4(4)	18(10)
Co-Ordinators	-	6 (11)	1(1)	7(3)
Promoting agency &Co-ordinators	-	9(7)	76(78)	85(46)
Bank	5(14)	-	-	5(3)
Promoting agency bank	19(54)	4(8)	-	23(12)
Multiple response	6(17)	13(25)	9(9)	28(15)
Nil	-	12(23)	8(8)	20(11)
Total	35(100)	53(100)	98(100)	186(100)
Internal factors				
Good leadership	1(3)	-	4(4)	5(3)
Co-operation	-	3(6)	2(2)	5(3)
Transparency	-	-	4(5)	4(2)
Multiple response	7(20)	15(28)	21(21)	43(23)
All the above factors	27(27)	35(66)	67(68)	129(69)
Total	35(100)	53(100)	98(100)	186(100)

Source: Field survey Figures in brackets are percentages.

Table - 6.21

Members' Perception on Factors Preventing Groups Further Growth

Factors	*MRD*	*CDS*	*Vikasama*	*All class*
Poor leadership	1(3)	-	4(4)	5(3)
Low educational Back ground	6(17)	9(17)	9(9)	24(13)
Lack of training/ Awareness/guidance	8(23)	9(17)	13(13)	30(16)
More financial assistance	6(17)	5(9)	13(13)	24(15)
Others	7(20)	9(17)	29(30)	45(24)
Total	35(100)	53(100)	98(100)	186(100)

In order to find out the factors, which hinder the groups growth and functioning the opinions of the members were collected. Table - 6.21 show that about one-third of the members. Irrespective of the groups, felt that farther progress is not possible because of poor infrastructure facilities. Even in some of the excellent groups, members expressed the need for better roads, bus and ferry services, brings across the Cauvery River and electrification of then ward. Absence of bituminized made and bus services force them to depend of private service operators (of jeeps and auto rickshaws) They felt that they could start small-scale industries or cottage industries, but the cost of transporting raw materials from KR market and taking back the finished products to the market is prohibitively expensive making their efforts un remunerative However 16 percent reported that absence of training and guidance prevented further growth of their groups. In MRD an equal preventive of members (23 percent) complained about poor infrastructure and lack of training and lack of training and guidance as factors standing in their way of progress 13 percent of the members of all the groups taken together remarked that they require more financial assistance for their groups further growth. A few members especially in Shreyas (30 percent) did not respond may be because they belonged to inactive groups or were dormant members not interested in the group's functioning and growth.

Impact of Self Help Group Movement on Women's Social And Economic Status

The membership to a SHG has contributed to significant changes in the lives of women. This was revealed by focus group interactions and field visits in the six towns undertaken for this study. Most of the groups visited could be assessed as successful in social and economic terms. Less than 5% of the SHGs formed under the program can be said to be defunct. Forty percent of the urban poor were covered by KUIDPS's SHGs in the short period that the project was active. The impacts can be looked at as those bringing in economic changes, impact on the social status and political impacts, and the impact of SHGs on the community.

Impact on Economic Status

Increased entrepreneurial skills: KUIDP convened a number of Entrepreneurship Development programs for SHG. Members which facilitated the learning of generic skills such as book keeping. This has allowed women to change from being wage workers to being self employed. Women also have gained the option to pursue two or three petty businesses, change from one type of business to another, combine wage employment with small business.

Increased access to credit: The micro credit facility of the SHG has encouraged women to save. They are at ease in their minds as they can avail money when they need, without having to pay any collateral. The most important effect has been the escape from the clutches of the money lenders. Pledging on jewelry has also reduced. The inters on loans has reduced from 120% per annum to 24%. They can request for adjustment in the duration of repayment.

Establishment of businesses: At lest half of the members (15-18- generally) have taken a loan from their SHG to micro-enterprise managed either by the women or by their families. There is an endless list of businesses established in this way, based on small credits of Rs.500 to sell flowers, vegetables and fruits, up to Rs.5,000 to establish petty shops and hotels, food grains, manufacture and sale of processed food products would need investments amounts varying between Rs.5,000 many women see housekeeping and child rearing along with earning for the family.

While vesting SHGs, the study found many examples that showed that the women who invested in businesses through their SHGs are better off. One woman visited, lakshmi, a member of Durgamba SHG at Mandya taluk had a save (traditional fabric worn by Indian women) business. At every purchase, she invested Rs.5,000 which the made a profit of Rs.1,300. The advantage in this is her be up with the traders of Mandya who were willing to take back the unsold fabric if any.

Woman now also have the opportunity to change from one income generating activity to another-suguna of Yeliyur SHG began with the sale of flowers but changed to selling of clothes which she found more remunerative. Many women gave benefited from the skill training programs and the entrepreneurship. The increase in income has allowed poor women to be able to prioritize their requirements and fulfill these. The general trend is to invest in business only after these have been fulfilled. A first priority is to educate the children. Women furthermore spent monies for health purposes, for house repairs and to purchase kitchen utensils. Some also cleared earlier loans that they otherwise would have to take with high interest rates. Many shifted from a rented house to a house on lease. It is only later that women also invest in purchase of consumption goods like televisions, telephones, and house sites.

Changes in consumption patterns: Food items were purchased once a week or once a month, as and when wages were received was done. This saved not only the time spent but also saved on amounts as bulk/wholesale purchases are priced lower than retail purchases and ensure better quality. There is a noticeable change in the consumption pattern and better household nutrition. The financial mobility due to participation in the SHG has led to an improvement in the quality of life, according to some of the successful groups. Overall, many families were able to address their basic needs better than before.

Impact on Social Status

This study found that the participation in the movement by it self as been an empowering and liberating experience for many of the poor women. The strongest impact has been in terms of self esteem and increased social mobility as many women of urban slums had never attended such a program before. The impacts can be summarized as follows.

(i) Increased mobility: This means a lot to poor women and to those who have been restricted by religious taboo. The visit to the SHG has made women more bold and confident Earlier, women were more confined to the four walls of the kitchen and some to the work place. They were now found to be able to meet each other and discuss problems.

(ii) Increased exposure: This comes from more interactions with other women. Women stated that they are more enthusiastic and positive about their lives. They understand each other's viewpoints and problems. Interaction with other women has resulted in building effect of spreading the SHG movement.

(iii) Increased awareness: Awareness on health related issues-personal hygiene, communicable diseases, effects of malnutrition and sanitation-have increased as a result of training programs. More importantly, awareness of the rights of women-as prescribed by the constitution and as prescribed by the religious doctrines-has also increased. The membership in the SHGs has allowed many women to come out of boundaries defined by their male companies or relatives. There are now cases submitted for legal mediation by Muslim women, something never heard of before.

(iv) Changes in decision-making, that affect their lives and that of their family household. They have more freedom to decide which of the meetings to attend and has much time they could spend without having to seek permission from the men and worry about the conflicts that might ensure at home as a consequence, Women also felt they have more say in the education of the children, such as which school children were to be sent to Men involved women in decision-making processes which were purely in the male domain before, such as house repairs

and the purchase of site, non inclusion of women in some major decisions that concern the household, have however continued.

(v) Increase in social security: Some of the SHGs have been successful in availing facilities like widow persons, old age pensions, health and the insurance for its members. This has resulted in the women feeling more secure about themselves and their future, Women abuse is said to have reduced and deserted wives have witnessed the husband return home. There are instances where SHGs have pressured men to put an end to violence/beating. This was revealed by the Focus Group Discussions held for this study. Physical violence has reduced in a few cases due to the collective pressure created by the SHGs. The unequal power relations between men and women, with the increasing economic power and social mobility of women, is changing However, many more changes are to be achieved, like achieving the rights of women to property, the reproductive rights and many more.

Summary

Many SHGs have helped in resolving family disputes. At Mandya, the incidence of harassment of a member of a SHG was resolved by joint efforts of women of three groups. A member was abused by the husband and the mother in-law who poured kerosene on her and threw her out of the house in the middle of the right of January 4,2005, Women members of three of the SHGs of the area went to her rescue and provided her with shelter and requested help of the NGO MYRADA. The NGO workers of Women help Line Program which MYRADA runs counseled the family members and have ensured that the mental and physical torture of women has stopped.

There are a number of less obvious benefits, in the area of soft skills, which are important in the context of women's empowerment. These are highlighted below

The skills of time management women have come to

value time more. For instance, cooking skills have become better time managed. Housework which was finished of leisure is completed within a short span of time (Gender division of labor at the household restricts women; men do not contribute to the household work of cooking, washing vessels, etc.,

Women have learnt to conduct meetings efficiently, both at the SHG and Federation level A few women in a group have also gained proficiency in maintaining documents and recording meetings. More importantly they have learned the skills of arithmetic which helps in the maintenance of books of accounts. By attending the meetings and training programs, women have improved their participatory and management discipline.

One of the mandatory programs of all SHGs, irrespective of who initiates, is the effort made to teach illiterates how to read and write. Having learnt and practiced this skill, many women feel more confident and less embarrassed when they are asked to sign their names.

Some women have learnt to speak new languages. The urban conglomeration is a mixture of different cultural groups speaking different languages, and the interaction between the women has facilitated the learning of new languages. In Mandya, the Urdu speaking Muslim women have learnt to speak in the local language. The skills of managing cultural events-organizing cultural programs and participating in cultural activities have been learn and practiced. The skills mastered by NGOs- that of forming SHGs has been picked up by many poor women. Women have facilitated formation more groups in both urban and rural areas.

7

Summary, Major Findings and Policy Implications

This chapter has two parts, part – I deals with major findings of the study and part – II deals with suggestion of the study. Twentieth Century is the independence of our country as well as of women. Women in India have made a considerable progress. Women's issues need to be focused upon since they have been neglected for centuries. Whatever our economy has achieved in whatever way it has been progressed in past 50 years, we could have probably done it 10 times better if women had been given equal status in society.

SHGs are aimed at poorest of the poor through savings and collateral free loan; the experiment has a long way to go. One needs to be cautions in replication and promotion of such non-formal organizations. They have certain limitations like small savings, inadequate loan, multiplicity of organizations trying the same model, lack of institutional support, linkages, problems of interference by politician's bureaucracy, long gestation periods, etc. If some of he above lacunas are corrected and meet measures initiated, it is hoped that micro credit would meet requirements of poorest of the poor in the country. This will also help easing government's efforts in providing reasonable livelihood to about one fourth of the Indian population.

Micro-credit movement has to be viewed from a long-term perspective. Its mission goes beyond development through credit for poverty eradication. SHGs led credit delivery system has shown seeds for a self-reliant economy inculcating business culture. It also develops concern for community development and brings social and economic mobility among poor women. This framework undermines need for a deliberate policy frame in terms of technology back up, efficient marketing network and human resource development. We need to avoid unfriendly regulations and over bureaucratization in controlling them.

Indian development planning has aimed at removing inequalities in the process of development to ensure that the fruits of development are an equal privilege of all sections of society. In recent years it has become increasingly evident that women are lagging behind a great deal both in availing of the benefits of development and as participants in the process of development due to several socio-economic cultural political impediments. The strengthening of women's economic empowerment requires actions in the area of recognizing women's right to sustainable livelihood and employment, all policies and programmes should be regularly undertaken, encourage policies for self-reliance, encourage economic empowerment of women, protect migrant workers in order to protect their dignity, and develop mechanisms to promote dialogue on policies and programmes of government organizations and non-government organizations.

It has been seen that SHG experiment got success in a few pockets of the country. Andhra Pradesh itself has 47.9 percent share of total SHGs formed in India. But there is an urgent need to spread this throughout rural India. By 2008, around 7 lakh groups were linked to the banks and around 5 lakh groups were refinanced by NABARD. The cumulative disbursement of loans to these SHGs was

Rs.2,048 crores. Fór the year 2008 a disbursement of Rs.1,022 crores was made indicating a rapid growth.

There are about 8,67,041 SHGs in the country emerging as a cost-effective tool of micro-finance for the financial sector. SHG-Bank Linkage Programme has linked financially 7,17,360 SHGs benefiting more than 11.6 million households by the end of March 2008. About 62,178 SHGs in Karnataka have been provided with credit of Rs.1,440.14 million rupees. Women borrowers and women SHGs have proved to be the most reliable and successful in this field. 90 percent of SHGs are women group, which is a significant factor in the direction of women empowerment and gender equality. NGOs and Rural Banks are playing a key role in providing better access to credit for the poor.

In Mandya district the SHG movement is good when we compare to other districts of the state. In Malavalli taluk all most all groups are matured, their saving motive is also good. In Mandya district data reveals that 74 percent of groups are functioning democratically. But norm regarding presiding of meeting by members in rotation is by only 18 percent of the groups. There is need to bring awareness about this norm.

SHGs' Bank linkage programme providing poor rural women with savings and credit facilities for setting up of expanding business, for investing in self-employment activities and for increasing household security. The popularity of SHGs Bank linkage programmes in India has been, in part, because of the belief that they will lead to poverty reduction and empowerment of rural women.

SHGs' Bank linkage programme enable the poor rural women to save and thereby improve their confidence and household security. Improved ability of the poor rural women leads to decreased dependence on moneylenders to borrow for consumption and production purposes.

SHGs have aimed at the poorest of the poor rural women to improve through savings and collateral free loan. The experiment has a long way to go.

Nevertheless SHGs have tremendous impact on the empowerment of rural women, they have certain limitations like small savings, inadequate loan, multiplicity of organizations trying the same model, lack of institutional support and linkages, problems of interference by politicians and bureaucrats, long gestation periods, etc. If some of the above lacunas are corrected and meet measures initiated, it is hoped that micro credit by SHGs would meet requirements of the poorest of the poor rural women in the country. This will also help easing the efforts of Government in providing reasonable livelihood to the poor rural women of the Indian population.

Part - I

Major Findings of the Study

Based on the analysis and discussion in the role of the Micro finance and its impact on livelihood security of women in Karnataka State in general and Mandya District in particular, the following findings have been drawn:

1. SHGs have potentiality to tackle the poverty and they can be an important weapon for poverty alleviation in Mandya district.
2. The study shows that there is an increase in the level of income and assets of the rural women of SHGs and reduction in the level of poverty as a result of intervention of micro finance by SHGs.
3. The net impact of borrowing on income is positive not only in case of all the borrowers but also in case of the poorest borrowers, showing the better outreach of the bank linkage programme. However, certain short comings are observed. Though there is positive impact on poverty, the process of empowerment is poor. Since these SHGs are women groups, the lower empowerment can lead to the failure of the programme in the long run.
4. It was observed that majority of women loaners belonging to economically weaker sections of

society, did not know the terms and conditions of bank loan including rate of interest, schedule of repayment and magnitude of installments. But it is very interesting to note that majority of the women of SHGs know about the opening up of savings bank account.

5. The main finding of the study is that Women Empowerment Programmes have made on outstanding impact on the women beneficiaries to undertake economic activities in Mandya District. The spread of bank offices has been spectacular and Women Empowerment Programmes have shown phenomenal growth during the reference period.
6. Self Help Groups has reached rural and urban areas of Mandya District satisfactorily and they helped them to livelihood security.
7. In Mandya district SHGs are forming in and around the taluks and mandal head quarters with a radim of 5 km.
8. The study indicates that the women who are involving themselves in economic activities and are able to earn independently are taking independent decisions in panchayat raj institutions.
9. A tendency has emerged among members to leave one group and join other groups, when the lanner are found more attractive. In some cases, the secretary of the CDS group was also the president of MRD, or vice verso. Instead of promoting healthy competition among the various agencies, the co-ordination and leaders consider other NGOs as their rivals. We suggest networking between groups and NGOs to facilitate smooth functioning. A co-ordinated effort of all voluntary agencies would pave way for overall development and solution of problems of infrastructure development and marketing and for putting an end to social evils such as early child marriage and dowry.

10. All the groups have taken up individual economic activities, but group activities are very few, there was apprehension among the leaders about the success of group enterprises because cases in which the group activity failed had led to financial imbalances and difficulty in loan repayment for all the members of the groups concerned. The situation was not so complex in the case of failure of individual units. It is felt that individual activity is better especially in the first two years until the group attains sufficient maturity and confidence in taking up group enterprises.
11. In our sample about 55 percent of the selected members in MRD 33 percent and 42 percent in Vikasama and CDS respectively reported to have taken up IGAs by availing micro credit. An attempt was made to examine the impact of micro credit on the beneficiaries. It was found that the contribution of micro enterprises to the total family income was 34 percent in MRD (almost one third) 25 percent in CDS and 27 percent in Vikasama. Thus micro crudity is seen to have credit a positive impact on the families of members. Factors other than investments made out of micro credit have also contributed to the increase in income derived from the activities of groups under MRD and Vikasama.
12. Members who had been carrying on some economic activity even prior to their jointing the groups were able to utilize the micro credit effectively for expansion and modification of their units and benefited the most. The impact in terms of production also differed according to their martial socio-economic status. Those motivated by the 'pull factor' were able to absorb credit more rapidly and put it to use in furthering productive activities. Since the opportunity cost was zero, any additional contribution to the family income may be

considered a positive impact. Their income generating opportunities were enhanced through addition to poultry and other activities, which the women found easy to manage in her homesteads and making use of their leisure time.

13. The main finding of the study is that Women Empowerment Programmes have made on outstanding impact on the women beneficiaries to undertake economic activities in Mandya District. The spread of bank offices has been spectacular and Women Empowerment Programmes have shown phenomenal growth during the reference period.
14. The study shows that there is an increase in the level of income and assets of the rural women of SHGs and reduction in the level of poverty as a result of intervention of micro finance by SHGs initiated by NGOs, which called for fuller realization of the promotion of livelihood security.

Part – II

Policy Implications

In the light of our findings and observations some suggestions are made about effective functioning of Self – Help Groups Micro Finance for livelihood security in women development. The suggestions are listed as follows:

1. The Governments both at the Centre and the State can think of the possibilities of implementing some of the subsidy / margin oriented schemes through the SHGs so that recovery performance and end utilization can be ensured besides reducing the transaction costs. Need is felt to arrange entrepreneurship development programmes for the members of the SHGs who are graduating themselves beyond consumptive credit to the production / investment credit. It could be specific skill oriented training.

2. In order to cover more and more weaker sections under this useful and effective rural development approach, it is required on the part of the government to implement as many development programmes as possible through the SHGs so that twin objectives like better utilization of the scheme and coverage of weaker sections can be achieved. Also, Government could earmark a part of the funds spent on providing subsidies under government-sponsored programmes for the formation of Self-Help Groups and providing useful incentives to SHG activity.
3. There is a need to introduce incentives for increasing the thrift activity among the poor. While some of the selected few groups among the government promoted groups get incentives in the form of revolving fund assistance, a large number of groups promoted by NGOs and banks need to get incentives. In view of this, incentives to these groups also may be provided through the banks where the accounts of the groups are maintained in order to increase their savings propensity. This also increases the proportionate credit dispensation to the rural poor through these groups.
4. In order to increase production levels of the SHGs significantly, the relevant production techniques and know-how need to be preserved and spread / shared among the production groups in order to standardize the production as well as packaging process that is suitable for storage and marketing. In this regard, the rural technology mission can be formed by the government with the involvement of the scientists involved in rural technology research, rural economists, rural bankers and NGOs involved in such activities.
5. The problem of promoting livelihood among SHG member is becoming increasingly important because of the need to create livelihood and employment

opportunities for higher incomes in the rural areas. We believe that the problem of rural migration, which is a cause of concern, could among others be addressed through this intervention.

6. It is important to note that most of the women beneficiaries are illiterate. Hence, the beneficiaries need to be educated about the formalities to be fulfilled in obtaining the necessary finance. The bank staff should help the uneducated women in getting their credit sanctioned from the banks. If the beneficiaries are educated they can get loans easily from the banks.
7. The NGO sector is increasingly pursuing the financial intermediation as one of the effective tools in meeting their social agenda. In this context, the governments, both at the centre and the states have an equally important role to play in creating conducive policy environment for the growth of this NGO sector as future micro finance institutions. Here, what is required is suitable policy framework, innovative package of services with timely credit.
8. Given the low levels of community and political participation by members, this aspect must be strengthened, since SHG members usually are people who are voiceless in the community.

Conclusion

Self Help Groups are playing a crucial role of harmonizing the society and strengthening rural economy and one of the major programme of poverty alleviation in India with full participation from the formal banking system and without any interference from the government.

Today's banking systems or processes are beyond the understanding of an illiterate farm women and the local money lender becomes her only sources of support. Since they get the money on time, women workers do not bother much about high interest rates. To put an end to this exploitation by private money lenders and at the same time give a status for the illiterate farm women in the society. Initially the women members had no income of their own for meeting their personal needs and depended on their husband's meagre income.

Personally, becoming a member of the self-help group has helped them. Previously, if they needed money urgently, they approached the local money lender or pawned some of their jewels. But now they are eligible for a loan of up to Rs.30,000 during an emergency. They are no long complicated paper procedures for giving the loan, which becomes available on verbal request of the members. They use the money to start their own income generating activities and the loan is repaid out of the profit they earn through the enterprise.

The present situation in the society to a large extent corruption in the development process, we can't totally rooted the corruption therefore we live with corruption, we adjust with corruption. The micro Finance and Micro Credit movements are growing rapidly but the achievement still limited, more concerted efforts needed to reach all the poor and especially of empowerment of women can be really achieved through self help groups.

From this study a number of important results have emerged. These results are in contrast to the findings of earlier studies. Some of the disagreements of this study with the early studies are: the income impact on the poor is higher, borrowers taking more number of loans and generate more income, larger organizations have larger outreach and formal schooling is an essential criterion for exerting better effect of Self - Help Groups on income generation. From the results of the present study it can be concluded that Empowerment Programmes have better outreach, positive impact on poverty, and employment generation on rural women. However, there is a need to improve the process of empowerment through the proper policy initiatives.

Bibliography

Anitha Arya (2000) Indian Women, Vol.2, Gyan Publishing House New Delhi.

Anjana Maithra Sinha (1993) Women in a changing society, Ashish Publishing House, New Delhi.

Karmakar K.G(1999) Rural Credit and Self-Help Groups; Micro Finance needs and concepts in India, Sage Publication, New Delhi.

Lalitha N. and B.S Nagarajan (2002) "Self-Help Groups in Rural Development", Dominate Publishers and Distributors, New Delhi.

Pillai J.K (1995), Women and Empowerment, Gyan Publishing House, New Delhi.

Reka Wagir (2000) "The gender GOP in Education-NGO as changing agents", Sage Publications, New Delhi.

Rose K. (1992) Where Women are Leaders: The SEWA Movement in India, Vistar Publications, New Delhi.

Susama Sahay (1998), Women and Empowerment approaches and strategies Discovery Publishing House, New Delhi.

Usha Sharma (1995), "Women and Society", Common Wealth Publishers, New Delhi.

Acharya, Meena and Lynn Bennett. 1981. "Rural Women of Nepal: An Aggregate Analysis and Summary of 8

Village Studies." The Status of Women in Nepal. Volume II, Part 9: Field Studies. Centre for Economic Development and Administration. Kathmandu: Tribhuvan University.

Ackerly, Brooke A. 1995. "Testing the tools of development: Credit programmes, loan involvement, and women's empowerment." IDS Bulletin 26 (3) : 56-68.

Balliwala, Srilatha. 1994. "The meaning of women's empowerment: New concepts from action." Pp. 127-138 in Population Policies Reconsidered: Health, Empowerment and Rights. G. Sen, A. Germain and L.C. Chen, eds. Cambridge: Harvard University Press.

Chen, Marty. 1992. Conceptual Model for Women's Empowerment. Unpublished.

DFID. 2000. Poverty Elimination and the Empowerment of Women: Strategies for achieving the international development targets. London: DFID.

Durrant, V.L. and Z.A. Sathar 2000. Greater Investments in Children Through Women's Empowerment: A Key to Demographic Change in Pakistan. Paper prepared for presentation at the annual Population Association of America meetings, March 2000, Los Angles, California.

Everett, Jana. 1991. The Global Empowerment of Women. Summary of the annual conference of the Association for Women in Development, November 17-19, 1989, Washington DC.

Hashemi, Syed M., Sidney Ruth Schuler, and Ann P. Riley. 1996. "Rural credit programs and women's empowerment in Bangladesh." World Development 24(4): 635-653.

Jahan, Rounaq. 1995. The Elusive Agenda: Mainstreaming Women in Development. Atlantic Highlands, NJ: Zed Books Ltd.

Jejeebhoy, Shireen J. 2000. "Women's autonomy in rural

India: Its demensions, determinants, and the influence of context." In Women's Empowerment and Demographic Processes: Moving Beyond Cairo. Harriet Presser and Gita Sen, eds. New York: Oxford University Press.

Kabeer, Nalia. 2001. "Reflections on the measurement of Women's empowerment." In Discussing Women's Empowerment-Theory and Practice. Sida Studies No. 3. Novum Grafiska ABL Stockholm.

Keller, B. and D.C. Mbwewe. 1991. "Policy and planning for the empowerment of Zambia's women farmers." Canadian Journal of Development Studies 12(1): 75-88 [as cited in Rowlands, Jo. 1995. "Empowerment examined." Development in Practice 5(2) : 101-107].

Kishor, Sunita. 2000. "Empowerment of women in Egypt and links to the survival and health of their infants." In Women's Empowerment and Demographic Processes: Moving Beyond Cairo. Harriet Presser and Gita Sen, eds. New York: Oxford University Press.

Mayoux, Linda. 2000. Micro-finance and the empowerment of women: A review of the key issues. Geneva: International Labour Organization. Available on-line at llo data/ public/ english/ employment/ finance/ download/ wp23.wpd.

Mehra, Rekha. "Women, empowerment, and economic development." The Annals of the Academy 554: 136-149.

Narayan, Deepa(ed). 2002. Empowerment and Poverty Reduction: A Sourcebook. Washington DC: World Bank.

Nussbaum, Martha. 2000. Women and Human Development: The Capablities Approach. New York: Cambridge Press.

Pitt, Mark M. and Shahidur R. Khandker. 1998. "The impact of group-based credit programs on poor households in Bangladesh: Does the gender of participants matter?" Journal of Political Economy 106:958-96.

Reeves, Hazel and Sally Baden. 2000. Gender and Development: Concepts and Definitions. BRIDGE Development-Gender Report No. 55.

Schuler, Sidney Ruth and Syed M. Hashemi. 1994. "Credit programs, women's empowerment and contraceptive use in rural Bangladesh." Studies in Family Planning 25(2): 65-76.

Schuler, Sidney Ruth, Ann Hendrix Jenkins and John W. Townsend. 1995b. Credit, Women's status and Fertility Regulation in Urban Market Centers of Bolivia. JSI Working Paper No. 8. Washington DC: John Snow, Inc.

Sen, Gita. 1993. Women's empowerment and human rights: The challenge to policy. Paper presented at the Population Summit of the World's Scientific Academies.

Stromquist, Nelly P. 1995. "The Theoretical and Practical Bases for Empowerment." IN Women, Education and Empowerment: Pathways Towards Autonomy. Carolyn Medel-Anonuevo, ed. Report of the International Seminar held at UIE, January 27-February 2, 1993, Hamburg, Germany. Paris: UNESCO.

UN Devision for the advance of Women (UNDAW), Department of Economic and Social Affairs. 2001. Empowerment of Women Throughout the Life Cycle as a Tran formative Strategy for Poverty Eradication. Report of the expert Group Meeting, 26-29 November. New Delhi, India.

Wedeen, Laura. 1996. Women's Empowerment in Nepal. Kathmandu: USAID.

Acharya,Sarathi: Employment of Women in India: A Historical review 1901-1951, vo1.22, Nov.3, October, 1979.

Agarwal Sushila: Status of Women, print well publishers,Jaipur.1988.

Agarwal,Bina(1985): Work Participation of Rural Women in third World,

Some Data and Conceptual Biases", Economic and political Weekly.

Ahmed.K:'Women's Higher Education: Recruitment and Relevance,Vikas Publishing House, New Delhi,1977.

Anker,R.Khan,M.e.Gupta,R.B.(1988):"Women's Participation in Labour force. A Methods Test in India' for Improving Measurement, International labour office, Geneva.

Ashine Roy,(2003): Women Empowerment and Gender Planning, Rajat Publications, New Delhi.

Atmanand (1990):"Women Labour force: Trend and Pattern Employment".Khadi Gramodyog, Vol.XXXVI, No.6,Mar,P.247-54.

Badal Chandra Das (2002): Rural Women in Micro-Enterprises: Concern and Challenges. Social Welfare, Delhi.

Banerjee,Nirmala (1989): trend's in Women Employment 1971- 81,Economic and Political Weekly, Apri1.29,P.20-21.

Banerjee,Nirmala,(1985)W omen Workers in Unorganised Sector, Hyderabad; Sangam Books.

Bhandari,R.L.(1982):Educational Development of India, Ministry of Education and Culture,New Delhi,P.36.

Bhatia.V.K.(1986):"Some Empowering Dimensions of Women Work Force", Manpower Journal Vol.XXII,No.2,july-Sep,p.31-44.

Bhoumik,K.L(1988),Development of Women and Children, New Delhi: Inter India Publications.

Boserup.E.(1989): Women's Role in Economic Development: Earth scan: London.

Chandrasekhar,R.(ed).,Women's Resource and National Development: A perspective, New Delhi, Gaurav Publishing House.

Charlton, S.E.M.(1984): Women in Third World Development, West View Press, London.

Chopra,Kusum(1978-79) :Role of Female Participation's in the Development and Relatively Backward

Chowdhary,P.(1992)Women Welfare and Development, New Delhi, Inter India Publications.

Das, Veena (1976) : Indian Women, work, power and status in Indian women, (Ed.) B.R. Namada, Vikas Publishing House.

Deepa Shrivastava (1998): Role of Women in Economic Development. Women and Economic Development Discovery Publishing House, New Delhi.

Desai, Neera (1974) : Women in Modern India, Vora and Company, Bombay.

Devasia Leelamma, Devaisa V.V. : (1994): "Empowering women for sustainable development" Manpower Journal, Vol. XXI Oct. Dec.

Government of India (1985): Seventh Five Year Plan, 1985-90, New Delhi.

Government of India (1992): Eighth Five Year Plan, 1992-97, New Delhi.

Government of India, (1995,1996,1998): Economic Survey, New"Delhi.

Government ofKarnataka (1995 to 2002): Economic Survey, Bangalore.

Gurumoorthy. T.R. (2002): Economic Empowerment Through Self - -Reliance. Social Welfare, Delhi.

King, Elizabeth, M and M. Anne Hill (1993): Women's Education in Developing Countries: Barriers, Benefits and Policities. The John Hopking University Press, Baltimore.

Kumar and Singh (1983) : Role of women in Rural Economy", kurukshetra, Jan. 13.

Lynn Bennet (1982): Women, Poverty and Productivity in India, World Bank, Washington D.C.

Mahajan .V.S. (1989): "Women's contribution to India's Economic and social development" Deep and Deep publication, Delhi.

Mathu,r, Deepa (1992) : Women Family and work, Rawat publication, Jaipur.

Raj Kumar Sen (1998): Optimising the Role of Human Beings in Economic Development. Women and Economic Development, Discovery Publishing House, New Delhi.

Regions of India,Center for the Study of Regional Development,Jawahar Lal Nehru univrsity,New Delhi.

Sarkar,Lotika,(1989): "Empowering Women" Seminar, 36(3), No. 19a9, pp.35-39.

Shrivastava, Deepa. (1987): Role of women in Economic Development of India, Annual Conference of Indian Economic Association, Rajasthan University, Jaipur.

Siddiqui, Mujibul Hasan (1993) : Women Education" Ashish publishing house.

Singh, C.P. and Mishra, R.B., Indian Women: Challenges' and change, Common Welath Publishers, New Delhi.

Singh, M. (1989) : Women and Development process in India", Khadi Gramodyog, Vol. XXXV, No.4 pa. 195-,205.

Singh. M.K. (1987) : participation of women in economic development trends and issues" Vol. 23, No.1, PP. 93-95, Industrial relations journal.

Tulasimala. B.K. (2004) : "Self help groups and economic empowerment ". Journal of social and economic development, Vol.

U.N.D.P. (1996,1997,1998): Human Development Report, Cxford, New Delhi.

Various Census Reports of Registrar, General of India.

Vyas, Anju and Singh sunitha (1993): Women's studies in India, sage publications. Wingnaraja, ponna (1990): Women, poverty and Resources, Sage publications.

Women Development Corporation Reports..

Zarina Batty: (1980): "Economic Role and Status of Women, a case sttudy of women in the Beedi Industry in Allahabad, world employment programme, working paper.

Ariz Ahmed M (1999), "Women Empowerment Self Help Groups", Kurukshethra, April, 47, 7-19-20 and 49.

Arun Kant Gautam and Priyanka Sharma (2007) "Micro Finance Intervention in North East India: An Assessment of SHG-Bank Linkage Programme" Punjab Journal of Business Studies, voi.3, No.1, April-September 2007.

Badal Chandra Das (2002) Rural Women in Micro-Enterprises: Concern and Challenges, Social Welfare, October.

Chirangee T (2003), Empowering Women Through Self Help Groups Experiences in Experiment", Kurukshetra, March.

Dodkey M.D (1999), " SHG and Micro Credit Sustaining Rural Women", Social Welfare, March.

Gangadhar.P.S (2002) "Micro Finance Initiatives: A Case Study of Bidar District", Research Paper (Unpublished).

Gurumoorthy.T.R (2002) Economic Empowerment through Self-reliance, Social Welfare, October.

Hoff, Karla and Joseph E. Stigliz (1990) Introduction: Imperfect Information and Rural Credit Markets - Puzzles and Policy Perspectives. The World Bank Economic Review, 4 (3):235-51.

Hulme, David and Paul Mosley (1996) Finance against poverty vol.I and II. Routledge Publishing, New York.

Kokila K (2001) "Credit GRO for Social Defense", Social Welfare May, 48;2,23.

Kopodia Karin (1997) "Mediating the Meaning of Market opportunities gender lost and class in Rural South India", Economic and Political Weekly.

Kumaran. K.P. (1997), "Role of NGO in promotion of self-help groups, Empowerment of people: Gross roots strategies and Issues", Kurukshetra March 1997, pp. 40-46.

Lalith N and B.S. Nagarajan (2002), " Self Help Groups in Rural Development", New Delhi, Dominant Publisher and distributors.

Lewis.W. Arthur (1955) The Theory of Economic Growth. George Allen and Unwin Ltd. London.

Lipton, Michael (1988) Foreword note in Rural Credit - Lessons for rural bankers and policy makers. Intermediate technology publications. London.

Mangathai R.A (2001) "Together we stand success Story" Kurukshetra, November.

Mani Mekalai .N and G Rajeswari (2002), groups roots Entrepreneurship through Self Help Groups (SHG). SEDMI Journal, vol.20, p.2

Mellor, J.W and B.M.Desai (1993) Institutional Finance for Agricultural Development. International Food Policy Research Institute, Washington DC.

Nair, Tara S. (1998), "Meeting the credit needs of the Micro Enterprise sector Issues in Focus", The Indian Journal of Labour Economic, July, September.

Narayana Swamy N.S. Manivel and B. Bhaskar (2003), "Net working SHG and Co-Operatives In Analysis of strengths and weaknesses", Journal of Rural Development, vol.22, p-3.

Nurkse, Ragnar (1952) Problems of Capital Formation in Underdeveloped Countries. London: Oxford University Press.

Padmanabhan,K.P (1988) Rural Credit - Lessons for rural bankers and policy makers. Intermediate technology publications. London.

Raj Mohan (2003), "Actives of Self Help Groups in virudhunagar District-A study "TNJC, pp.25-29.

Renu Verma (2008) "Micro finance and Empowerment of Rural Women", Kurukshetra, September 2008 p.p3-5.

Resure R.A(2003) "Women Empowerment Through SHG" Journal of Fact for yojana, November.

Ritu Jain (2003), " Socio-Economics Impact Through Self Help Groups", Yojana, vol 47. N.7. pp.11-12.

Rose R. (1992), "Where women are leaders the SEWA Movement in India', New Delhi, Vistar Publications, (An division of Sage Publications India).

Sabya Sachi (2003), "Self Groups and Micro Credit Synbergic Integration", Kurukshetra, vol 51, No.10, pp 25-28.

Sankar Datta (2009) Consolidating the Growth of Microfinance, Economic and Political Weekly, July 25,2009, Vol.XLIV No.30.

Siddiqw Saif (2003), "Rural Entrepreneurship and poverty Alleviation Programmes", Yojana, December.

Siraman. V.P. (2006), "Micro Finance, Self-help groups and Women Empowerment current issues and concerns", working paper 38.

Sybyolachi Dos (2003), "self-help groups and micro credit", Kurukshetra, August 2003.

Von Pischke, J.D (1980) Finance at the Frontier: Debt Capacity and the Role of Credit in the Private Economy. EDI Development Studies, The World Bank. Washington DC. Articles Published in News Papers

'NABARD initiatives turn rural women into entrepreneurs', the Hindu, Feb 20, 2004.

Where HLL Shakti comes from the Hindu Business Line', May 29,2003.

The Schwab foundation for social entrepreneurship, the Hindu, January 24,2005.

Microfinance Banking for the poor and not poor banking, the Hindu, January 24 business line, March 15, 2005.

SHG movement takes a leap forward, the Hindu, September 30,2005.

Gearing up SHG to create a silent revolution, the Hindu, November 10,2005.

SHG women get computer Draining, the Hindu, November 18,2005.

Women SHG fewer in western India Expert, the Financial express, January 21, 2006.

Micro credit looking beyond group, lending, the Hindu, Business line, April 14, 2006.

Index

A

Abstaining from leadership, 101
Activity status, 110
Administrative structure, 79
Age group, 102
Agency-wise
  cumulative participation in Karnataka, 72
  distribution, 102, 104
Agriculture, 69
Alternative micro-finance institutions, 34
An overview, 28
Area, 69
Assuming leadership role, members perception, 100
Attendance, 93

B

Background, 28, 77
Bank linkage, physical and financial progress, 74
Banks in Karnataka, micro-credit lent by, 70
Block-wise
  literacy details, 83
  population details, 81

C

Case study analysis, 92
Changes in consumption pattern, 117
Clavey loams, 78
Credit, 96
Cultural characteristics, 78-79

D

Decision-making, 53
Demographic profile 81
Development process, gender perspective in the, 53
Development skills in women, 61
District, 80

Distribution of members, 106-07, 111

E

Economic
- action, 62
- empowerment strategies for, 57
- empowerment of women, 53
- national policy for the, 17, 48-62
- status, impact on, 116

Economy, 58, 62
Education action, 61
Empirical studies, 22
Establishment of businesses, 116
Evolution of microfinance, 30
Expected outcomes, 58
Exploitation of women, 60

F

Factors
- behind group success, 112
- contributing to group success, 114
- preventing groups, 114

Failure, 112
Female workers, characteristics of, 59

G

Gender justice, 1
Gender-wise population details, 81
Generate awareness among women, 61
Globalisation, 55
Goals, 51
Group meeting, 93
Group size, 93
Group-wise activity status of beneficiaries, 108

H

Historical profile, 81
Hobli-wise revenue villages, the details of, 90

I

Importance place, 79
Increased access to credit, 116
Indian experience, 40
Industry, 56, 79
Introduction, 16, 49
Irrigation, 69

L

Language, 78
Leadership, 98
Level of education, 107
Literacy, 68
Literacy scenario, 85
Literature, 78
Living, standard of, 69

M

Major findings, 17, 21
Major findings of the study, 124
Mandya district
  general particulars of, 86
  geographical details of, 85
  population of, 87
  taluk-wise area of, 87
Meanstream microfinance institutions, 33
Micro
  credit, 54
  empowerment of women programme, 17, 77
  finance, 40
  finance institution in India, 42
  programme, 17, 77
  programme in India, 16, 28-36
  programme in Karnataka, 17, 64
Monthly family income, 111
Motivating factor-members perception, 92

N

National policy on micro-finance, 35

O

Objectives, 51
Occupation, 79
Other general information 80

P

Policy
  implication, 17, 121, 127
  prescription, 52
Poor, livelihood needs of the, 72
Population, 68
Problems, statement of the, 11
Provisional population, details of, 88

R

Reasons for introduction, 36
Record maintenance, 94
Red
  clavey loams, 78
  sandy loams, 78
Research gaps, 26
Review of literature, 16, 19-26

S

SC and ST population, 68
Selected members, 102
Self help group movement, impact of, 115
Setting, 1
SHG bank
  in Karnataka, 69
  linkage programme, 46-47
SHGs in Karnataka, 17, 64, 76
Social status
  distribution of members by, 115
  impact on, 117

Socio-economic, 78
  development of women, 17, 77
  profile, 102
Source of data, 15
Study
  chapter scheme of the, 16
  hypotheses of the, 15
  methodology of the, 15
  objective of the, 14
  scope of the, 13
Summery, 17, 47, 74, 119, 121
Support services, 56

T

Theoretical framework, 19
Thrift, 95

W

Women, 56, 58, 62
Women empowerment, 1
Women welfare, 1
Women's
  contribution on economy, 59
  social and economic status, 115
World of work, 60